I0016250

Scrum Project Management

Avoiding Project Mishaps

Beyond the Basics

By

Gary Metcalfe

The following book is reproduced below with the goal of providing information that is as accurate and reliable as possible. Regardless, purchasing this book can be seen as consent to the fact that both the publisher and the author of this book are in no way experts on the topics discussed within and that any recommendations or suggestions that are made herein are for entertainment purposes only. Professionals should be consulted as needed prior to undertaking any of the action endorsed herein.

This declaration is deemed fair and valid by both the American Bar Association and the Committee of Publishers Association and is legally binding throughout the United States.

Furthermore, the transmission, duplication or reproduction of any of the following work including specific information will be considered an illegal act irrespective of if it is done electronically or in print. This extends to creating a secondary or tertiary copy of the work or a recorded copy and is only allowed with an expressed written consent from the Publisher. All additional rights reserved.

The information in the following pages is broadly considered to be truthful and accurate account of facts, and as such any inattention, use or misuse of the information in question by the reader will render any resulting actions solely under their purview. There are no scenarios in which the publisher or the original author of this

Table of Contents

Introduction

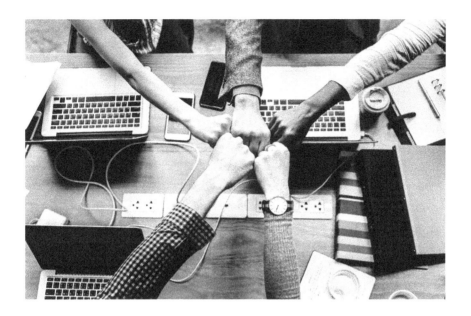

Congratulations on purchasing *Scrum Project Management* and thank you for doing so.

Are you looking for ways to improve the efficiency and productivity of your team without having to do a bunch of training or spending a lot of money on outside help? Are you interested in reducing your costs when it comes to producing a new product? Would you like to find a way to include more customers to the process and to provide them with a better customer experience? If any or all of these pertain to your business, then it may be time to consider implementing Scrum into your business model.

The following chapters will discuss everything that you need to know about the Scrum Framework and how to make it work for your own needs. Many companies are looking for a way to reduce their overall risks when it comes to developing and releasing a new product. They are looking for a way to reduce the costs that they incur when producing a new product. And they are looking for ways that they can get their employees to work together and become more productive and efficient overall.

There are different methods that can be used to make all of these happen, but none are going to be as efficient as working with the Scrum Framework. This guidebook is going to take some time to talk about this framework and all that it can do for your company.

This guidebook starts out by talking about some of the basics of the Lean methodology, the Agile Framework, and more and how they relate to Scrum and can benefit your business. We will then move into some of the basics of the Scrum framework, spending time on what Scrum is about, some of the different roles that are needed with Scrum, some of the benefits of using this method, and even how the sprints work and how the team can utilize their time the best with all of this put together.

At the end of this guidebook, we will also spend some time looking at a few different examples of how to work with Scrum so that you can see exactly how the Scrum Team would work with this framework and all the great results that it can yield. Many companies are worried about implementing this kind of framework because they think that it will cost too much, will take too much time, or it will just be too hard for them to implement. But when you see these tutorials and learn more about the Scrum Framework, you will see that it is such an easy process that can really improve the way you do business and you will wonder why you didn't implement it before.

When you are ready to learn more about the Scrum Framework and how it can really make a big difference in your business and the way things are done, then make sure to go through this guidebook to help you get started!

There are plenty of books on this subject on the market, so thanks again for choosing this one! Every effort was made to ensure it is full of as much useful information as possible. Please enjoy!

Chapter 1: What is Lean

Before we are able to get more in-depth with the idea of Scrum and how it works, it is important to understand a bit of the Lean process. This is a process that helps businesses to be more efficient, serve their customers better, and can reduce the amount of waste that the company produces. Many companies who are experiencing issues with customer satisfaction and those who are worried about how many returns and broken products they are dealing with will implement the lean principles to see some vast improvements in their business. This chapter will help introduce Lean to you so that we know what we are getting into when working with Scrum.

To start, Lean is a customer-centric methodology that a business is going to use in order to continuously improve their processes. Most companies will start with just one process to improve and make better. This gives them a trial run of the Lean methodology and then they can move on to other processes and to implement this methodology in all aspects of their business.

The point of using the Lean methodology is to improve a process in the company by eliminating waste in everything the company does. It has many different steps and options to make it successful, but some of the main ideas that come with this methodology are respect for people and continuous incremental improvement.

The basic principles that come with Lean methodology include:

- The company needs to always focus on being able to effectively deliver value to their customers.
- The company needs to be willing and able to respect as well as engage the people.
- You should use Lean to help improve the value stream because you can learn where waste is occurring within the business and how to eliminate that waste.
- Lean is there to maintain a good flow through the business.
- Lean is there to help add more pull through the system.
- Companies who use Lean are striving to reach perfection.

In the Lean methodology, you are going to let your customer tell you what they value. As a business, you are not there to tell your customer what they should like or what they should come to expect from you. Instead, the customer is going to define the value of your company. There are three conditions that you need to consider when making a new product or when you want to add something new to an existing product. The three conditions include:

- The product or feature needs to be done correctly the very first time.
- It needs to be something that the customer wants and will actually spend their money on.
- The feature or the method needs to be able to transform the product or service.

If you don't meet with all three of these criteria, then you are just dealing with waste or activities that are not valuable to your company. And one of the main things that you are going to work with when it comes to the Lean methodology is how to cut out waste easily and effectively.

So, we have spent a little time talking about waste in this chapter. Lean is very much about identifying and then eliminating as much waste out of your business as possible. Many companies have a lot of waste in them which can cost them a lot of time and money down the drain, can make customers dissatisfied with the company, and just makes them inefficient overall. Waste in a business is going to show up in three main forms including Mura, Muri, and Muda.

Mura is simply going to be waste that occurs because of the variation in how a product is handled. Muri is going to be any waste that happens when you stress or overburden the system, equipment, or the people in the business. But Muda is known as the seven forms of waste or the seven places where it is likely waste is going to occur in your business. The seven most common forms of waste in a business that Lean is going to work to solve will include:

- Transportation: You should look at your business and see if there is any movement of information, materials, and parts between various processes that are really unnecessary and taking up time.

- Waiting: Do you notice that there are a lot of people, systems, facilities, or systems idle because they are waiting for the work cycle to finish?
- Overproduction: Are you producing a product faster, sooner, and in larger quantities than the customer is demanding?

- Defects: Does the process result in anything that the customer would not be happy about or would send back to you?

- Inventory: Do you have any finished goods, work in progress, or raw materials that are not getting any value added to them?

- Movement: How many times do you end up moving goods, equipment, people, and materials within a processing step?

- Extra processing: How much extra work is performed beyond the standard that the customer requires from you?

Every business, no matter how big or small could benefit from some of the principles that come with this methodology, although sometimes, the costs of implementing it are too high for some smaller companies. Either way, the lean methodology is important to ensure that you learn how to provide a high-quality product that the customer wants without having to deal with all the waste that is common for many businesses.

Lean is also a great way to define and then improve the value stream of your business. This value stream is going to be all the information, people, materials, and other activities that need to flow and then come together to ensure that the customer is getting the value they want, when they want it, and how they want it. You can identify this value stream using a value stream map with the right icons in place.

You can also work to improve your value stream by doing a plan-do-check-act process. The 3P methodology that includes production, preparation, and process is going to be used up front to help you design products and processes before they reach their final form. By creating an environment of safety and order, you are going to find that it is much easier to identify where the waste is happening.

There are many different parts that come with the Lean methodology, but it is basically there as a way to help companies learn where some of the major waste in their business is and then helps them to get rid of this waste so they can get products done that the customers will enjoy, without wasting time or money. It benefits the customer because they get an amazing product that they want and it benefits the company by saving a lot of time and money.

Chapter 2: What is Agile Framework?

Now it is time to take a look at the Scrum Agile Framework! At this point, you may be curious about what this even means. You may worry that it is something that is inside a fancy computer program or something that high-level management or computer programmers will work with. But is that what this system is all about? Yes, this term is a bit complicated and confusing, but it is actually a lot easier to understand than you might realize. This chapter is going to spend some time looking at the Agile Framework and discussing what it all means to Scrum.

What is a Framework?

First, we need to start with the basics. A framework is a term that software development will use and it is there to provide solutions and functionalities to a particular problem area. Basically, it is when you have the "framework" there already, but then the user or even you do something to alter it and to help you. A good way to think about this is if you make a cup of tea each morning. You will put in different ingredients into the cup every time and you don't measure it out. On one day there is more sugar and on another day, you may add honey. It doesn't really bother you that much because, at the end of it all, you are still going to get your cup of tea.

But then there is one morning, you think of an idea that could help make you more productive with things. Instead of having all the ingredients separately, you measure out the correct ratio that you want to use for one cup of tea and then you place all of the dry ingredients together in one container. From then on, every morning, all that you need to do is scoop out a spoonful and you will end up with the correct amount of everything you'd need without having to measure it out again. It can save time, it can make things easier, and you end up doing less work in the process.

This is exactly what a framework is going to do for you. Using a code for your computer, you or someone else can change up the framework to make it suit your specific needs. It can help make productivity better and make things easier than before.

What is Agile?

Now that we have a good idea of what framework is about, it is time to look at the other part of our term, the Agile part. Agile itself means the ability to move easily and quickly. But how are we going to use this information and apply it to the framework that we talked about before? Agile Framework is specifically going to refer to the method of project management that will be used in software development and it is often characterized by the ability to turn tasks into shorter phases of work.

Basically, instead of just working on one project that is tedious and long, the Agile Framework is going to take that long project and break it down into smaller parts. This helps out because everyone can focus on one small thing at a time, ensuring better focus and more quality control. This kind of framework is going to be based on 9 different principles which are basically there to inform and then inspire the roles and practices of Scaled Agile Framework. The 9 principles of Scaled Agile Framework or SAF include:

- Take an economic view: One of the biggest reasons that you would consider using this kind of framework is because it is going to provide you with the highest quality product at the best value in the least amount of time. However, being able to do this requires that you have an understanding of the economics of your building systems. Your daily decisions need to be made using the right economic context or they will fail.

- Apply systems thinking: The systems that you are going to work with are complex. There are a lot of components that will work together and each one is going to have shared and defined goals. To improve this, you need to make sure that everyone is committed and fully understands what the system is used for. Systems thinking should be used in the building system of your organization.

- Have some variability in mind and ensure that the options are all preserved: A big sector of design practices will favor just one type of design and the qualification options at the beginning of the developmental process. If you do a wrong take-off, it is going to end up having a big effect. This is going to generate a project design that will be too long-term for you to handle. Be aware that some variability needs to be implemented in your process for the best results.

- Build in increments with fast and integrated cycles of learning: To make sure that you don't deal with a long-term product is to make sure that you develop some solutions that have short iterations through them. The iterations will build from the one before it and can allow you to have a faster input from the customer, leading to fewer risks. Iterations can sometimes turn into prototypes that are used with testing out the market. You then rely on some of the early feedback to determine whether you want to keep things as they are or make any alterations that are necessary.

- Let milestones be based on a fair assessment of the active systems: Customers, business owners, and developers need to regularly evaluate the system to assure it is going well. All these groups share the responsibility to ensure that the investment in the chosen solution is going to economically benefit the company. This is why it is so important to have those integration testing points in place. Doing this can help you have some milestones that can be used by everyone to perform evaluations and make sure the developmental life cycles stay on track.

- Conceptualize and then reduce WIP, batch sizes, and then see the lengths of the queue: The entire point of using a system similar to this one is to ensure that you reach a state of continuous flow so you can allow new capabilities in the system to visibly and quickly move. There are three points that you need to consider that will really help the workflow you are dealing with including:

- o WIP: This stands for work in process. It is important for you to conceptualize and reduce the WIP status. This is then going to reduce the requests for unnecessary changes in the process.

- o Reducing the magnitude of your batches can make it easier to produce a flow that is not only fast but also has some reliability to it.

- o Doing something about how long your queue is can be a great way to hurry up the time of fresh tasks.

- Make sure of cadence. Time it with the cross-domain planning: Cadence is important because it is going to help create a good predictability and rhythm for development. When you apply it to the idea of synchronization, it is going to allow for many perspectives even ones that are different, to be understood, and the issues waiting for simultaneous attention and integration. When this all happens, the team is more effective even if there are periods of uncertainty during developing the product.

- Open up the inner encouragement of dispensers of ideas: The pursuit of knowledge, innovation, and ideas won't ever happen if your workers don't have any motivation. This becomes even more of a problem if you hand out compensation individually because it can cause some internal competition and gets rid of any cooperation that you need to achieve your goals. Providing some autonomy and purpose can help engage your employees more which helps to provide great outcomes for you and for your customers.

- Decentralize the decision making: This type of decision making is going to be required when you need to achieve fast and valuable delivery. This can help to reduce delays, gives you even faster feedback, can improve the flow of development, and encourages more creative solutions. When a decision has to be run by those who are higher up, this is going to cause more delays in the whole process, adds more setbacks, and can cost the company more money. When everyone is involved in the same kind of decision-making hierarchy, the development process is going to stay smooth and easy.

So, why would you or another business want to use the Agile Framework? Yes, we talked about a few benefits above, but you may consider your current process as working well and you don't want to change things up. But let's look at an example of how this can work.

Let's say that you are working on a project and it has been taking you a long time. You finally get done with that product and show it to the customer, but then your customer decides they don't like it or they would rather have different features. This means that you have to go back through the whole process again and change a ton of things again wasting productivity and time along with lots of money.

With the Agile Framework and the SAF principles that we just talked about, you will be able to handle this problem without all the waste, without the wasted time, productivity, and money. Working with this is going to include the customer, the developmental team, someone in charge, the stakeholders, and anyone else who is a part of this process. This helps you to streamline your work, lets you have some input from your customers, and can ensure that you fix the product early on so that when it is finally released to the general public, it is the exact product your customers want.

Chapter 3: The Most Important Things to Remember About the Agile Framework

While it is very important for most businesses to learn how to streamline their work to save time and money, the world of Agile Framework is going to consider other rules as more important and more necessary. This kind of framework is going to concentrate more emphasis on a community, on the customer, on working together, and on accepting the fact that there will be changes along the way. This means that your business and your team need to have the ability to go with the flow.

The Agile Manifesto was created in order to ensure that other businesses and companies that used the program would implement it for the right reasons. The four rules that come with this Agile Manifesto and which must be followed include:

- Individuals and interactions are over all the tools and processes
- Working software over comprehensive documentation
- Customer collaboration over contract negotiation
- Responding to change over following a plan.

Any time that you decide to work with the Agile Framework, it is important to remember those four rules above and to figure out the best ways to implement them into your work. When you think about these rules, remember the utmost target is essential. This is to meet the aspiration of the clients and not just with your end product, but even when you are in the early parts of developing that product.

To help you do this, try to welcome the various changes you encounter even if they do start to happen later on in development. Agile Framework is able to use the acceptance of change in order for the customer to get a competitive advantage with that product.

It is also important for you to deliver some working software as often as possible. The range may be from a few weeks to a few months based on the type of software that you are working with, but it is always preferable if you can stick with the shortest timescale possible. You will also notice that the actual developers are important to this kind of framework. These developers are going to help build up the projects and when these individuals are motivated, it leads to much better results. Provide these developers with all the support they need along with a good environment and trust that they are going to succeed if you want to get the best results.

The Agile Framework is going to be a bit different than what you may have seen with some of the other business models out there. It forces you to implement a lot of different people into the plan including customers right from the very beginning. But this can do wonders for your product. We will discuss how this process works a bit later. But basically, you can get quick feedback at all the developmental stages of your product in order to make changes right then and there, rather than completing the product and then finding out you have to start from scratch. Working with the Agile Framework and Scrum will ensure that you can get this done!

Chapter 4: What Does Scrum Mean and How Does It Fit In?

Now that we have spent some time in this guidebook talking about the Lean methodology and the Agile Framework, it is time to take a look at Scrum and how it can fit into all of this. There are going to be some different approaches to using the Agile Framework, different methods, and types that the user can work with based on what works the best for them. Each approach or each type of agile framework is going to be considered lightweight. What this means is that all the practices and the rules for each approach are going to be kept down to a bare minimum.

In addition, each approach will also need to ensure that the main focus here is on empowering your developers to make good decisions together and to collaborate with each other. You will notice that each developer who works on this framework is going to come into the project with a different background which can be great news for allowing the group to work more effectively and quickly. You never want to end up with a group of people who all know how to do exactly the same thing. Having a group of people with different backgrounds and knowledge can help you create a team that is more cohesive and more ready to get things done.

As we go through here, it is important to remember that the big idea of working with the Agile system is to create all your products, applications, and more in small increments. Each of these individual increments is tested before you can consider them complete. This assures that the product is built with quality at that time, instead of trying to waste time finding quality later on down the road.

Remember that the Agile Framework is going to be a process that your developmental team is able to follow to ensure that only positive things occur. It has been designed to make it so all parties, both your business and the customer, can provide feedback while the project is being developed, rather than after the product is done and has gone to the market. Doing this can cut out a lot of problems that may creep up and actually makes your business and your process more efficient in the long run.

And while there are quite a few different choices that you can make when it comes to software development approaches in this framework, the most popular ones that many people choose is Scrum. Scrum is a framework that has a broad application that allows users to manage and control incremental and iterative projects of all different types.

Scrum can be really useful if there are many different types of projects that you need to complete at the same time and it will ensure that your team is able to complete each of these projects in a timely manner. At the same time, Scrum will work to make sure that the value of your product doesn't end up changing at the same time. The philosophy behind Scrum depends on connections and collaboration which can ensure that your team completes each of these projects in the best way possible.

To make sure that all of this can be done, there are several different roles that come with the Scrum process and each person on the team needs to be willing to take their role seriously. If even one person on the team doesn't do the job the right way, then the whole process is going to fail. Remember that Scrum is all about staying connected and about team-work.

To break it down even more, there are three basic principles that come with the Scrum ideology including:

- Adaptation
- Inspection
- Transparency

The Scrum ideology is all about seeing how things are and making sure that everyone on the team knows what is going on as well. It's important that you be concise and clear as much as possible and that everyone is always informed. It may be tempting at times to hide mistakes, but this just leads to a ton of issues down the road when other team members don't know what is going on. Transparency is so important during every step of this process to ensure that everyone is held accountable.

Scrum is also going to require inspections to help everyone and everything stays on track. Without this, it is hard for the team to know if they are even working on a project that will hold value for the customer and they may get to the end and find that the product doesn't even work.

And of course, we can't forget all about adaptation. Things are going to change —that is just a part of life. It's important for your Scrum team to be able to adapt to all the different changes that this process is going to go through. The customer may change their mind, the team may decide that they want to change up the way they will complete a task, and the Product Owner can make some changes to the Product Backlog.

Each product will go through a ton of changes throughout its process and being adaptable can make these changes easier to handle. If there is no adaptability when it comes to this process, the product is not going to be created and the entire process must be reworked.

More about Scrum

Scrum is basically a framework where people are able to address many complex adaptive problems, while still being able to creatively and productively deliver products that have a high amount of value for their customers. Scrum by itself is just a simple framework that can be used to ensure that team collaboration occurs effectively even on a complex product. Scrum is a great framework to use because it is simple to understand, can take some time to master but is worth the time, and lightweight.

Scrum is simple and is the opposite of a big collection of interwoven mandatory components. It is not a methodology like some of the other Lean ideologies that we talked about before. Instead, this framework is going to implement the scientific method of empiricism. It is going to replace a programmed approach with a heuristic one, with respect to self-organization and people to help deal with any unpredictability and when it comes to solving complex problems.

If you are looking to implement Agile into your business and your programs, then Scrum is probably the framework that you are going to work with. This is such a popular framework that many people think that Agile and Scrum are the same things. You can easily use other frameworks to help implement Agile including Kanban, but many times Scrum is preferred because it is easy to work with and it has a nice commitment to doing smaller iterations of work.

What is So Special about Scrum

With Scrum, there are a lot of things that you are going to enjoy about the framework and how it can make your product work better. The product is going to be built in a series of fixed-length iterations which are known as sprints which can give teams a framework for dealing with software on a regular cadence. Milestones, which are also the end of a sprint, are going to come often. This helps you to feel like there is a tangible amount of progress with each cycle. This quick movement can make team members feel like they are meeting goals and can provide a form of energy to the work.

Short iterations in the Scrum framework are going to help reinforce the importance of good estimation and some fast feedback from tests will help you know if you are taking the right direction on the product or if you need to try something new.

When you are working with Scrum, you are going to need to call up four ceremonies. These four ceremonies are going to bring structure to each sprint along the way. These four ceremonies are going to include:

- Sprint planning: This is going to be a planning meeting that the whole team needs to attend. During this time, you need to determine what you and the team want to be able to complete in the coming sprint.

- Daily stand-up: This is known as the daily Scrum. This is going to be a short meeting, about 15 minutes, where the software team can get together and sync up to know what to accomplish that day.

- Sprint demo: This is a sharing meeting where the team can get together and show what they were able to ship that sprint.

- Sprint retrospective: This is a review of what went well with the process and what didn't go so well. You can use this information to ensure that the next sprint goes a bit better.

During your sprint, some visual artifacts such as burndown charts and tasks boards will be visible to everyone on the team and can be some powerful motivators. They can show each person of the team how far everyone has come and can even be used to show off new work during the sprint demo to motivate people even more.

Three Important Roles for Scrum Success

A Scrum team can often have a different composition than a traditional project and you will see that there are three main roles that need to be covered. These three roles include product owner, development team, and scrum master. And because these Scrum teams are cross-functional, the development team is going to include engineers, designers, and testers in addition to all of your developers on that project.

First are the product owners. These are the champions of the product. These individuals need to focus on understanding all the market and business requirements and then will take this information and prioritize the work that needs to be done by the other groups. Products owners who are the most effective are able to:

- Manage and build up the backlog of the product.
- Work closely with the team and the business to make sure that everyone understands the items that are in the backlog and what needs to be done.
- Provides the team with clear guidance on which features need to be delivered next.
- Decide when to ship the product with a slant towards delivering more quickly.

Keep in mind that the project manager and the product owner are not the same people. Product owners are not going to be in charge of managing how the program proceeds. Instead, the product owner is going to focus on making sure that the team is able to deliver the most value to the business. Also, the product owner needs to be just one person. Even if there are technically several people who can hold this role, it is best to just pick out one individual who can do the work. You do not want your development to get guidance from several product owners at once. This slows down productivity and can just make things more difficult to handle.

Next on the list is the Scrum master. These are the champion for scrum within the team. They are going to be in charge of coaching not only the team but also the business and the product owner on how the Scrum process works. They should also spend some time learning how to fine-tune their own practice of it. An effective Scrum master really understands what work the team is doing and can ensure that the team optimizes their deliver flow. As a facilitator in chief, they are going to be there to schedule the logistical and human resources, planning out sprints, stand-up, sprint review, and even the spring retrospective.

The Scrum master is also going to take a look and figure out how to resolve impediments and distractions for the development team, insulating them from external disruptions whenever possible. Part of the Scrum master's job is to make sure that there aren't any anti-patterns that start to show up. One that is pretty common with teams that are new to Scrum is when the team tries to change the scope of the sprint after the sprint has begun.

It is pretty common for a product owner to ask "Can't we get this one more super important little thing into this sprint?" This may not seem like a big deal, but it can quickly snowball and will put you behind your schedule. Keeping your scope airtight will help you to keep on track and can be great for product planning. Plus, it is going to fend off some of the disruption sources that occur with the development team.

Scrum masters are sometimes thought of as the project managers, but these types of managers don't have much of a place in the Scrum methodology. The Scrum team can often handle itself and will organize around their own work. Agile teams are going to use a pull model where the team is going to pull a certain amount of work from their backlog and then will commit to completing that work during the sprint. This can be a great way to maintain quality and can ensure that the best performance is going to come out of its team over the long-term.

In this process, neither the product owners, project managers, nor scrum masters are there to push work on the team. They will list out the work that needs to be done, help to direct some of the things that should happen during the sprint, and more. The team gets to do a little bit of self-regulating in this process which can increase morale and provides higher quality work for the business.

And to finish the team out, there is also the Scrum team. These are the ones who will work on sustainable development practices. The Scrum team that will be the most effective is co-located, tight-knit, and between five to seven individuals. The team members need to have a different set of skills so that they can cross-train each other. This ensures that there are more effectiveness and productivity in the team and ensures that one person doesn't become bottlenecked with the process. They will often learn how to use the Scrum methodology in order to get things done for the business.

All three of these parts need to work together in order to make a product as successful as possible. You need someone who can list out the work that needs to be done by the team, you need someone who can avoid the distractions and keeps the team on task, and then you need the actual team who is able to do the work. When all of these different parts are able to work through this well, you will see that a business can become more effective and productive than ever before.

Chapter 5: What is Scrum Good For and What are Some of the Benefits of Implementing This Ideology?

Now that you have had a little introduction to Scrum, you may be interested in what this is good for. What can you use this Framework for and why would you even want to use it in the first place? Is it even worth your time at all or should you choose to go with something else?

There are a few different reasons why Scrum can be so good for your business and it is definitely a great idea to implement it in the way that you do business. The first one is the factor of competitiveness. The market around you is changing all the time and only those who are able to keep up with the trends and be flexible are able to keep up with all of this change.

Using Scrum, your business is going to stay competitive and can create a unique advantage for yourself. And you can get all of this through the solid and successful Agile Framework, a Framework that has proven itself throughout many teams and projects over time. Militaries, colleges, and even the automotive industry use Scrum so you know it could help your business to succeed.

Scrum has also allowed the development of features that can help your customers stay involved as well. The customer is able to use this framework to receive some of the working versions as they are designed through the process, look at some of the progress that is being made, and even add in some new ideas if they need to. All of this is important because you never want to wait until the product is 100 percent done before showing to the customer or you increase your risk of something being wrong or something not being the way that the customer wants and your sales will plummet.

Working with Scrum involves the customers to ensure that you are providing them with the product that they want to enjoy. You can always complete prototypes and show them off to the customer, taking in feedback, and making changes as necessary. Then, when you are ready to release the final product to the main market, you can rest assured that the product is actually something that the customer is going to want to use.

Another big part of working with Scrum is the quality. Testing is something that your Scrum project needs to have happened after every sprint. And since sprints can last no more than four weeks, this testing is going to be done on a daily basis. Doing this is going to ensure that the quality of your product is kept high from the beginning to the end. And if any problems do occur, they can be fixed right away.

The Scrum Framework is also going to help with the costs that your business incurs which is something that you are going to love as a business. Each project is going to get a fixed period of time to get done which means that the cost for it is set from the beginning and won't go higher. And while the effort, as well as some small details, can change, the cost is going to remain the same because the project has a deadline that can't be extended.

Your customers are also going to love Scrum because changes are something that is always welcome. These changes can be given to the product owner at any time of the process and then that product owner will follow through with them when the next sprint meeting occurs. The product owner can share this information with the team who will then implement the changes as soon as they can, sometimes within the next day depending on the length of the sprint and the type of change that is needed. Doing this can ensure that the customer is able to get a product that they really want and a happy customer is always good news for your business.

Another thing that Scrum can help out with is to increase the amount of efficiency in creativity and communication skills throughout the business. It requires that everyone who is working with the project is able to communicate, collaborate, respect, and understand each other. A successful is built off what the team develops and what the customer wants and Scrum is a great way to enforce both of these in your business. Those who are on the team are going to benefit a lot from getting these communication skills, but they are developed over stages so that in time, they will be able to communicate in a way that is very effective for them.

The development of complex systems and extensively long projects can be frustrating and difficult at times. However, Scrum is able to help with the exact planning that is needed for these projects. In the process, this allows for the integration of new functionalities and a new way of thinking about things. Using Scrum is a great way to make things run smoothly and ensures that you don't get to the complete end of a project before finding out that something has gone wrong. It can streamline the process for you, which always makes things better for everyone.

You will also find that working with Scrum once you get some of the basics down can even be fun. It is a great collection of teamwork, making decisions, and collaboration. Many people find that once they get to know the other members of the team, it can be nice to work closely in a group like what is required with Scrum. It can help you to learn new things, use your creative side, and challenge yourself while still having a support group there to help and encourage you along the way. Using Scrum means that you are able to implement the best part of software development which is a creative and multi-faceted activity that is going to work its best when each member of the team takes the time to do their fair share.

There are also times when Scrum can be helpful in specific ways for a business. After all, maybe you look around and find that your business is doing well and you aren't even certain that a change is needed after all. However, one thing that you need to consider is that organizations and companies that implement Scrum often experience some changes in the whole culture of their company.

What this means is that you will notice some changes in the ways that people interact with each other, how work gets done, and even loyalty from your employees. Companies that implement this system become more team-oriented, place more value on their customers and are more value oriented than ones that never use Scrum. Think about it from the eyes of your employees. Would you rather work for a company that only takes a look at their bottom line and the profits, or is it better to work for a company that genuinely cares for its people? Businesses that use Scrum teams show more high performance and will show results that are way higher than normal teams.

But what about on the other side of things? We just talked about how a business that is doing well may still want to implement Scrum but what about those companies that are in deep trouble and who want to adopt the Scrum system. They may worry about doing this because of the shaking up the new system may do. But Scrum is going to shake things up in a good way by helping allow a new team environment, a new process, and a new culture that can do wonders for helping the business get out of the trouble they were originally in.

With these businesses, sometimes a big shake-up is exactly what they need to turn things around. They can make these changes to the work environment, which helps make it easier to retain the right employees, which translate into better work, which then translates into products that the customer actually wants to purchase. In this scenario, the most important thing is that a business needs to openly admit that they need help. This can be hard for some companies, but the longer you hold onto this denial, the more bad things that are going to happen down the line for the business. Using Scrum can help the business get back on their feet, out of the deep trouble, and back to the place where they would like to be.

You will most likely find that implementing Scrum into your work or business won't be too difficult. You do need a Scrum Master along, but the training for that doesn't take too long or you may consider hiring someone into the company to hold this position if that works better. Then, you must make sure that everyone on your team is on the same page and understands how this Scrum Framework is going to work, why you are going to implement it for the new projects that the company is going to work on, and what you expect from everyone who is on the team.

Once everyone on the team is on the same page, you will quickly find that Scrum will make all of the differences that we are talking about in this guidebook. It can help you to make a great product that your customers love. It can improve morale with your customers and gets many of them to feel more connected with the projects that your company needs to work on. And with the shorter sprints that are recommended in this guidebook, it is often a great way to keep motivated with the team. Instead of them having to wait months to get the full project done, they can break it up into the smaller sprints, none of which should be over four weeks long (and many are often shorter time frames). The team members can start to see instant results in some cases for the work that they are doing which can be a great motivator for them to keep on working.

Another way that you may be able to use Scrum to help out your business is when there is a small business that has a high-performance state but has trouble maintaining this high performance when they want to grow at the same time. This kind of company can easily implement some of Scrum into their organization to balance things out. Scrum can make it easier to streamline the production so that this smaller company isn't overwhelmed as much even though there is a lot that is going on. The organization helps immensely in all these situations and can make the end goal seem easier to accomplish.

Of course, while we do spend quite a bit of time talking about companies and businesses that could benefit from Scrum, anyone who is trying to work on a complex problem or project can find that this framework is a great one to use. It could be someone who is working on a new smartphone app, someone who is looking over a store or a charity event, or any other complex project. Scrum is also a great way to turn your to-do list into tasks that can be managed, to help improve the teamwork that is necessary between all the parties, to create fast results, and to improve communication skills. These can be great benefits whether a big organization or an individual person is using the Scrum framework on their project.

Now, we spent a lot of time talking about the various benefits that come with implementing the Scrum framework into your business. If those reasons weren't enough, here are seven more reasons that are going to show just how great Scrum can be and can make the decision to change over to the Scrum framework easier than ever before. The other seven reasons that you may want to consider Scrum include:

- Perfect implementation: Scrum has a defining set of roles, rules, artifacts, and activities that come with it. When you use everything together, you then end up with the ability to implement your ideas in a way that seems almost perfect. As long as the team is able to keep with every rule and role, then the project is going to turn into a streamlined process that you will love to use.

- Easy to use: Scrum is actually really easy for your team to use and you can introduce it into your organization with a minimal amount of hassle. Even though there are several roles that need to be filled and there are some regulations that you need to make sure that everyone follows, one person isn't going to take on all the responsibility. It is going to be spread out through the entire team which can ensure that no one gets stuck with all the work and makes life easier for everyone.

- Flexibility: Scrum is great because it is such an adaptable practice. Sometimes you don't always start out with all of the information and you will end up gathering it along the way. This will result in some changes being introduced during the next sprint and implemented in as well. This is something that Scrum can handle so it doesn't become a big deal when a change is necessary.

- Reduces a lot of your risk: Since you spend your time working in increments, you are able to use Scrum to help reduce some of your risks. In doing these increments, the cost of development will be reduced and the risk of starting over after putting in all the time and effort will be lowered. The traditional methods of business where the team spent months or more working on a product and then hoped that it did well at the end of everything are gone. This is very risky and takes the customer out of the process too much. With the help of Agile and Scrum, you are able to keep the customer involved the whole time. Then, when it is time for your final product to reach the market and the mass public, you have the confidence that you are providing a high-quality product to the customer that your customer actually wants.

- Optimize team efficiency: Scrum is very much about a team that is able to work together well in order to get the tasks done. By following the right stages and resolutions, the Scrum Team can become a very unstoppable force that can create a ton of different ideas in the process.

- Customers get the chance to use a product before it is officially released: When you are done with every sprint meeting, there will be a sprint review done. This is where your customers are going to be introduced to the new features and changes that you implemented into the product and the customer gets to try them out. This part of the project is usable to the customer, allowing them to inspect your teams' work and try it out. Doing this will lessen the amount of work that your team needs to do at the end of the process, while also ensuring that there is some quality control that goes into it all.

- Continuously improving: When one project is done, your team is going to move into the sprint retrospective. This is when the team is going to meet up and then discuss any constructive criticism or other issues that may happen or did happen during the timeline of that project. When the team takes the necessary time to figure out any issues at that moment, rather than putting them off and not thinking about them, they can ensure that no similar issues happen in the future.

As you can see, there are a ton of implementations and benefits of using the Scrum Framework. It is important that everyone is on board when it comes to using this system and that everyone is willing to listen, communicate, and work together during the sprints to get the work done. If only one person does all the work or even if one person refuses to do any work, it can throw off the dynamics of the whole team.

But with all of the benefits that come from using the Scrum Framework and all of the efficiency and productivity that it can give your team, it is still a great option to use and many times, you won't run into any troubles getting your team on board with this new method of getting things done on each project.

Chapter 6: Non-Core Roles in Scrum

In the last chapter, we spent time talking about some of the important roles that are needed in the Scrum system. There is also some non-core roles that you need to consider for your team. These are not mandatory roles like the other three and you may start the process without them if needed, but they are still important because they can play a good part in the project. Some of these roles include the Scrum Guidance Body, the Vendors, and the Stakeholders. Let's take a look at these different non-core roles that can help make your Scrum project more successful.

Stakeholder

The first non-core role we are going to take a look at is the stakeholder. This term is going to be used in order to include users, sponsors, and customers who are able to work with the Scrum Team, Scrum Master, and Product Owner. These stakeholders have the job of coming up with ideas and helping to start the creation of the product or service for the project and they can also provide some influence throughout the development process for this project.

The customer, in particular, is the one who is going to purchase the product or service when it is all done. It is possible for the project to have customers that are inside that same organization also known as internal customers, or you may have customers who are outside the organization also known as external customers. Both of these customer types can do a great job when it comes to helping you with the Scrum project.

Then there is the user of the product. Just like with the customers, you can also have external and internal users. It is even possible that in some cases the users and customers are going to be the same person. And finally, the sponsor is going to be the organization or person who is able to provide the needed resources and support for the project. They can also be the one who is accountable for the project when it ends.

Vendor

Another non-core role that can come with Scrum includes the vendors. These are going to be outside organizations and persons in the project. They can provide products and services that are not usually found within the project organization. They can help bring in items, resources, and more that may not have been available before.

Depending on the type of project you decide to work on, you may find that you will need to work with a vendor. They will be able to provide you with the materials that you need to complete the project. Make sure that you build up a good working relationship with the vendors you need to ensure that you can always get the products and supplies that you need to keep your project going smoothly.

Scrum Guidance Body

The Scrum Guidance Body is another optional part that can come with your project and it is going to be made up of either a group of experts or a group of documents. This guidance body is going to define government regulations, security, objectives that are related to quality, and other parameters that are needed as the project moves on.

These guidelines are important in helping the Scrum Team, Scrum Master, and Product Owner to finish their work in an effective and consistent manner. This guidance body can be a great way for the organization to know the best practices to follow and which ones they should use in all their Scrum projects. You don't want your team to spend a lot of time working on a project to find out that it doesn't match up with what the company values the most, what the regulations for the company outline, and with government and federal regulations for all companies.

This guidance body is going to come in and make sure that the organization knows what the best practices are and which ones should be used in all of your Scrum projects. If you or your team ever has a question about the regulations and rules of Scrum and you want to make sure that you meet all these, then talking to the Scrum Guidance Body is a good place to start to ensure that you stick with all these rules.

One thing to note about this guidance body is that it is not there to actually make decisions that are related to the project. They are not there to decide what tasks to work on, how to work on the tasks or anything else that the Scrum team or others may focus on. Instead, it is there to make sure that all guidelines are followed. It will use guidelines in a structural way for everyone in the project organization to consult the program, project, and portfolio. Your Scrum Team can find that this is a good place for them to start on all projects and they can ask the guidance body for advice when it is needed.

Remember, these roles are not all necessary and you may be able to work on your project without these roles. You and your team can easily keep track of the supplies that you need to do and you can even work on the regulations and more on your own if needed. These extra roles can be really nice if you are able to afford to have them along, but if you can't, then you can easily keep your Scrum team working and doing well without them.

Adding these three non-core options to your team can help you become more efficient and can get the projects done easier than before. Many teams can do well with just the core positions that we discussed before. But other companies find that adding these parts, at least part-time, can really make a difference in how their project will go.

Chapter 7: The Different Parts That You Need for a Successful Scrum Project

Now it is time to take a look at what the different parts are that you need to add to your Scrum project. These are often called artifacts and the Scrum Framework is going to use these in order to ensure that they can provide some accurate information about a product. This could include information about what happens to the product while it is being developed, the different activities that are being planned for the product, and even what activities the team already did. There are a lot of different artifacts that are used in a Scrum project, but some of the most important ones include,

The Backlog

User management	Travel reservations	Promos and offers
Create an account	Book space travel	Percentage discounts
Stored payment info	Book a hotel	Companion flies free
Linked family profiles	Book rental space	Customer loyalty
Travel preferences	Book group tickets	Family discounts

The first artifact that we need to talk about for our Scrum Framework is the backlog. This is going to be a list of the features, fixes, functions, and requirements that are needed for the product for any of its releases in the future. As the product is released to the market and customers start to use the product, feedback will be sent back to the team and the changes that are put in the backlog are going to get even bigger.

When you first release a product, the backlog is probably going to be small or have nothing in it. At most, you may find that there are a few ideas that the team wanted to explore but didn't have time for. But when that product is first released to the market, the backlog will remain empty. Over time, as customers use the product and start to provide feedback, the backlog is going to start filling up a little more and you will notice that a lot of new tasks will be present on this as well. The number of tasks will depend on what the feedback for the product is, what other products you want to work on, and how long you go between the original release and a new one.

It is even possible for the team to go through and change the backlog completely, depending on the market conditions, business requirements, and technology. As long as your product exists, the product backlog is going to change, adapt, and exist as well.

In most instances, the items that are on your product backlog are going to have a description, estimate, order, and value assigned over to them. This list is never going to be a finished one and it will constantly change depending on what needs to be done or changed to the product at the moment.

Often, the product owner is going to be the one person in charge of this backlog, though it is possible for the team to create something that is known as "Product Backlog Refinement". When this happens, the Scrum Team has added priority order, details, and estimates to the list and they have made decisions on how and when the refinement needs to be done.

The process of refinement of a product is very important and it can determine what activities get chosen and how the product changes over time. Some of the different activities that occur during this refinement process will include:

- Reviewing the items that are considered the highest priority at the top of this backlog.
- Asking for more information about this project if needed. The Product Owner would have the answers that are needed.
- Deleting any items that are no longer relevant.
- Writing in new items when needed.
- Ranking and prioritizing the items that are on the backlog
- Redefining and accepting new criteria as it is needed.
- Refining items that you need to prepare for some of your future sprints.
- Understanding that the architecture of a product can change as your backlog starts to emerge.

The more details that you are able to put into this backlog, the higher up on the list it will go. This is so important to have precise estimates on each item in order to get the project completed. So, if an item has fewer details, it is going to be lower down on the list and it will take the team longer to get to. Once the Scrum Team is able to put more details on the item, it is possible for that one to move up higher.

Sprint Backlog

The next thing that you can work on with this framework is the sprint backlog. This is kind of like a to-do list of tasks that the Scrum team needs to get done. It is a set of items from the original backlog that are selected for that particular sprint and will include a plan to ensure that the goal is done during that sprint. Basically, this backlog is going to show the Scrum Team what they need to get done to ensure that they meet the goal of that sprint.

This is a list that can see some modifications through the process though. If there is new work that shows up, the Scrum team will need to add it to this backlog. And in some cases, the team will look at the list and deem some of the tasks as unnecessary and they will take that item from the list.

Only your Scrum Team can make any alterations to the sprint backlog during that sprint. It is made to specifically help the team and can ensure that they stay on track and focused. It is like a real-time picture of the work that your team needs to accomplish during a particular sprint and it is important that the team has full control over everything on it.

Sprint Burn-Down Chart

In many instances, this won't even be considered one of the artifacts, but it does show up quite a bit during the process so it is still an important thing to talk about here. While a sprint is going on, the team is able to track the amount of work that is still remaining on their sprint backlog. This is one of the best ways for the team to see how long they have to achieve their goal and can make it easier for them to manage the progress they are making.

Many scrum teams are going to use a practice that is known as the Sprint Burn-down chart as their method to monitor this progress. The product owner is able to take this information and will compare it over with other sprint reviews. This helps them to see if the team is on time and going to complete the work in time in order to reach the goal. Then the product owner can share this information with their stakeholders and other interested parties to help everyone be on the same page during the project.

Increment

The increment is going to be one of the most important artifacts with the Scrum Framework. The increment is when the team can combine all the items of the product backlog that are completed during a sprint with the increments of all the previous sprints. When one sprint ends, the increment needs to be considered complete which means that it now is in usable condition and also meets the team's "Definition of Done". The definition of done is a document of shared understanding by the team that will define specifically what they mean when it comes to being done with a sprint.

Now, every Scrum team is going to have a different definition here and often it is going to change and mature as the team starts to grow. And even though the product owner may decide not to release it at that time, the product needs to at least be in working conditions. The members of the team need to be responsible for defining what is considered an increment. There can be some different opinions here, but they all need to have an understanding of what it means for the work to be complete in order for that product to be officially done and ready to go.

The team is then able to use this information once that task is done. This information can also be useful when the team needs to know how many items are selected from the original backlog during sprint planning. The team can decide how long the sprint is going to take, how much work they want to take on, and when they consider the product and the sprint to officially be done for them before moving on.

The main thing to take away from here is that the product backlog and the sprint backlog are going to be used in order to tell the team what work needs to get done and all the work on those backlogs need to add value to the final project. The product increment is when the product is completed through its sprint. Each of these parts is going to serve a specific purpose to make sure that everyone on the team is working together, that they have a good idea of how to be on the same page, and that the team can complete the right tasks to reach a common goal in the end.

Chapter 8: How the Product Backlog Works

An agile backlog that is well-prioritized is so important. It not only helps to make release and iteration planning a bit easier and it also broadcasts all of the items and works that the team is going to spend their time on. This can include a lot of internal work that the customer will never even see. This backlog is going to help set some realistic expectations with stakeholders and any other teams that are involved, especially when it comes to those teams trying to bring additional work to your team and can make engineering time more of a fixed asset than it was before.

What is the Product Backlog?

There are a few different types of backlogs that you will see with a Scrum project, but here we are going to spend some time looking at a product backlog. The product backlog is going to be a list of work that has been prioritized and ranked. This is work that the development team can choose from to work on and it is derived from the roadmap and all of the requirements that come with this. The most important items that need to be done first are going to be shown at the top of this backlog, alerting the team as to what they need to deliver and get done first.

The development team doesn't need to work through this backlog at the same pace as the product owner. The product owner is also not going to push work to the development team so this process gets rid of some of that pressure and stress. Instead, the development team pulls work from this backlog as they have the time for it and then get it done. Basically, the team will get ready to plan out a new sprint and decide how much of the work they can effectively and realistically get done within that sprint time.

The team's roadmap and their requirements are going to form a lot of the foundation that occurs in the backlog of the product. The initiatives of the roadmap are going to be broken down into what are known as epics and each of these will have several user stories and requirements.

The product owner is then going to take each of these user stories and organizes them into a single list that is easier for the development team to look over and choose from. The product owner can sometimes choose to deliver the full epic first or they may decide to release it all with the most important items first and let the development team works from there.

The product owner gets to choose which items are the most important and need to be done first. They will handle the ranking system to save the development team some time. Some of the factors that will influence a product owner's prioritization include:

- Customer priority
- Symbiotic relationships between work items
- Relative implementation difficulty

- The urgency of getting feedback

While the product owner is going to be the one responsible for ranking the different work items in the backlog, they do not do this all on their own. Effective product owners will seek feedback and input from designers, the development team, and customers in order to optimize the workload for everyone and to ensure to get the best product delivery.

Making Sure that the Backlog Stays Healthy

Once the backlog is built and ready to go, it is important that the product owner maintains it on a regular basis to ensure that it is keeping pace with the product. The product owner needs to go through and review the backlog before each iteration planning meeting to make sure that the rankings are still right and that new tasks haven't been brought in that need to be ranked higher than some older options. They can also look to see if the feedback that came in from the previous iteration is now incorporated into the product backlog or not. This regular review of the backlog is called backlog grooming in agile circles or it can go by the name of backlog refinement.

Once the backlog starts to get bigger, the product owners need to group the backlog into long-term and near-term items. The near-term items need to be fully fleshed out before they are labeled as such. This means that the user stories need to be drawn up, collaboration with the development and design teams need to be sorted out, and estimates from the development team are drawn up and ready to go.

The longer-term items, on the other hand, don't need to be done right away. These can remain vague a bit, but it is a good idea to get some estimates from the development team to make things easier down the line. Remember that the key thing to remember here is "rough". The estimates are going to change once the team fully understands and starts to actually work on these items that are long term.

The backlog is going to serve as the connection between the product owner and the development team. The owner is free to go through and rank the work in different ways based on any customer feedback, refining estimates, or new requirements that come up. However, these changes need to be done before the work is in progress. Once the work is considered in progress, or the developmental team decides they are going to include it in their sprint, it is best to keep changes away as much as possible. Every change can disrupt the flow of the product and can affect focus and morale at the same time.

There are also some patterns that are going to make things more difficult and that you need to watch out for. Some of these include:

- The product owner prioritizes the backlog at the start of the project but they don't make adjustments as the feedback starts to come in from the stakeholders and developers.

- The team limits items that are on the backlog to those that are only customer facing.
- The backlog is kept as a document and stored locally. It is also not shared often so it is hard for the people who are most interested in it to get the right updates along the way.

How can this Backlog Help my Team be Agile?

Good product owners are going to spend time on the backlog, making sure that it is a reliable and sharable outline of the work items that need to be completed for a project. Stakeholders, at times, will challenge some of the priorities and this is not always a bad thing. Fostering discussion around what is the most important can get everyone's priorities in sync. These are good discussions, ones that are going to foster a culture of group prioritization that ensures that everyone is on the same page when it comes to working on the program.

This backlog is also the foundation when it comes to iteration planning. All of the items that need to be completed should be on that backlog. This includes items like action items left from the retrospective, customer requests, technical debt, design changes, bugs, and user stories. When all of those items are in one place, it ensures that the work items are included in the overall discussion for every iteration. Team members can sometimes make a trade-off with the product owner before starting an iteration, while also knowing everything that must be completed in the end.

The product owner is the one who will be in charge of dictating the priority of all the items that need to be done through the backlog. The development team is then going to dictate the velocity or the speed that they can get through this backlog.

This can be a hard thing to get used to for some newer product owners who wish to push work over to the team, but it ensures that the team has more power and say over what they can do and avoids them getting overworked and losing morale in the project. If something needs to be ranked higher or changed along the way, the product owner can always move that to the top of the list to ensure it gets done a bit faster.

The backlog is going to be an important part of the Scrum project. It lets the product owner decide what needs to be done first and what items all need to be done to start with, and it allows the development team to pick what items they want to work with over the next sprint. Everyone gets to feel some ownership in the cycle and there isn't an issue with the team feeling overwhelmed from all the extra work their product owner is sending to them, while the product owner gets the benefit of knowing that the work will get done. This brings a lot of harmony and goodwill to everyone on the team.

Chapter 9: Understanding How Sprint Planning Works

We have discussed a bit of the process that comes with the sprints, but now it is time to take a look at the particulars and details about sprint planning. Sprint planning is basically an event in the Scrum process that kicks off the sprint. The purpose of doing this is to define what the team is going to deliver during that sprint and how that work is going to be achieved. This kind of planning needs to be done in collaboration with the whole Scrum team.

In Scrum, the sprint is going to be a set period of time in which the team needs to get all of their goals done. They will go through the product backlog and pick the tasks and items that they wish to work on the most and then move on from there. However, before you are able to get to work and be in action, you need to take the time to set up the sprint. You must decide how long the sprint is going to be (it can be anywhere from one day to four weeks), the goal of the sprint, and where you plan to start.

The planning session is going to kick off with some agenda setting and some focus exercises. If it is done the proper way, it can also make sure that the environment for the team is where they are challenged, motivated, and have a chance to be successful. If the sprint planning is bad, then it can sometimes derail the team because they set unrealistic expectations and just can't get all of the work completed.

There are a few things that need to be considered when it comes to good sprint planning sessions. Some of the questions that are often asked and answered by the Scrum development team during this time include:

- The what: The product owner will start out the planning session by describing the goals or the objectives of the sprint and what items in the product backlog are going to contribute to that goal. The team will then decide what can be done during that sprint and what steps they are going to take throughout the sprint to make sure they can get all of the work done.

- The how: The development team is then going to plan out the work that is necessary to help them deliver the goal of the sprint. The resulting sprint plan is going to be a negotiation between the product owner and the development team based on value and effort and what can be done during a specific amount of time.

- The who: You can't get through sprint planning without both the development team and the product owner. The product owner can be important because they are going to define the goal based on the end value that they want to achieve. Then, the development team must understand fully how they can, and sometimes can't, deliver on that goal. If either party is missing from this planning session, it becomes very hard to plan out the next sprint.

- The inputs: A great point to start for the sprint plan is the product backlog. This is basically the list of work items that need to get done and some of them are going to become an important part of your current sprint. The team should also take some time to look at any of the existing work that was done during that increment and then checks out the capacity to see where they need to go from there.

- The outputs: The most important outcome of this kind of meeting is that at the end, the team is able to describe the goal of the sprint and how they plan to take steps to work towards this goal. This is something that is going to be made visible in the sprint backlog.

How to Prepare for a Sprint Planning Meeting

Running a great sprint planning session can take some discipline. The product owner needs to be prepared. They need to have information about the previous sprint, feedback from the stakeholders, and a vision for the product because all of this information can help them set the scene for this sprint. To help with any issues to transparency, the product backlog needs to be as up to date as possible and even have some refinements as needed.

The refinements to the backlog are more optional, mainly because there are some backlogs that are not going to need to do this step. However, for most teams, it is best to get everyone together and do a review of the backlog and even complete some refinements before they get started with sprint planning.

If you are working on a two-week sprint, you may want to work on a refinement meeting for the backlog in the middle of that sprint. This is a great time because the team can take a step back from their sprint for a few minutes and look at what is going to come in next. This can prepare you ahead of time for sprint planning but sometimes provides another perspective when it comes to the current work the team is doing.

Set a Time Limit for the Planning Process

Sprint planning should not waste up a time. You should never take up more than two hours for each week of the sprint. This is probably a bit long. A two-hour meeting for a two-week sprint is probably enough. This process is often known as timeboxing or setting a maximum amount of time for the team to get the task done. For this situation, we are setting a maximum amount of time that the team can work on planning out the sprint.

The Scrum Master is the one who is responsible for making sure that this planning meeting happens and that the timebox is understood. If the team is able to get through the work quickly and the planning meeting is done before the timebox finishes, don't sit around wasting time. The timebox is all about a maximum amount of time that is allowed but there is never a minimum as long as all the tasks are assigned properly and everyone knows what they should be working on in the end.

Focus on the Outcomes, Rather than the Work

During this sprint planning, sometimes it is easy for the team to become kind of bogged down in the work. They will spend too much time focusing on the task that needs to come first, who should do the task, and how long that task is going to take. For a complex amount of work, the level of information that you know in the beginning will be low and often a lot of that is based on assumptions. But with Scrum, you are working on an empirical process. This means that you can't plan upfront, but that you are going to concentrate on doing and then you will feed that new information that you have back into the process.

The goal of the sprint is going to describe the objective of the sprint at a high level, but the items in the backlog can often be written with an outcome in mind to make things a bit easier. User stories are an example of this because they will describe the work that needs to be done from the point of view of the customer. User stories will help refocus any defects, issues, and improvements on the outcome the customer is seeking, rather than on the problem that has been observed.

By taking the time to add in measurable and clear results to this user story, it is much easier to measure the outcomes and then you will have a clear idea of when things are done. You want to gather this clarity as much as possible upfront, can make it easier to get started and do well with this product. For example, you will find that leaving things vague in the product backlog is a much worse problem compared to describing something as a question to be answered at some point during the sprint.

Remember that not knowing a fact is a completely different situation compared to being vague. You don't need to ignore the unknowns because they are simply a reality of doing work that is difficult. But never hide them behind vague words. Instead, it is better to be clear when you don't know something and then frame the work in a way that the team will try to gain an understanding about that topic or that item.

Estimates are Required But Never Pretend to Know More Than You Actually Do

As you start to get into sprint planning, you will find that there are times when you need to estimate something. The team will need to define what can or can't be done in a particular sprint so they will estimate how much they are actually capable of doing. Estimation is sometimes confused with a commitment to this process.

Estimates are going to be based on the knowledge at hand. Techniques such as story points can add in some value to this process because they allow the team to find new ways to look at a problem. However, these estimations are not meant to be magical tools that will find out the truth, especially if there is no truth to find out. The more unknowns are in the process, the less likely that the estimate is going to be the right one.

A good estimation requires an environment of trust, an environment where information is given freely and where any assumptions are going to be discussed in a way that can help the team to improve and learn. If these estimates start to be used in a negative or a confrontational way after the work is done, then it is more likely that the future estimates are going to either be too big (ensuring that the team isn't wrong again), or the time taken to make them will be much longer (the team second guesses itself because they don't want to deal with any implication of the guess being wrong).

During this planning session, your team should explore some of the different techniques that can be used to help do estimations. You may find that using some different techniques can provide a much different view of the problem than before.

The Best Practices for Sprint Planning

It is sometimes easy for a team to get bogged down in all of the details that come with this kind of planning. Remember that instead of focusing on all the little details, you need to focus on creating a "just enough" plan for this sprint. This plan should focus the attention of the team on valuable outcomes and will allow for good guardrails for self-organization. A good plan for a sprint is going to motivate the whole team because it defines an outcome along with a clear and good path for success.

But you also don't want to spend too much time planning a lot upfront. This can get in the way of all the work and the items that need to be done later on. Instead of building up a plan that accounts for every minute the whole time, you should focus on a plan that has a goal and one that has all the tasks in line so the team knows what they are working on. Also, make sure that the product backlog is still ordered and ranked so if the team does happen to get done with the goal of the sprint early on occasion, they can go back through and pick up more work if needed, rather than just sitting around wasting time.

Basically, during the Scrum planning process, it is your job to get things organized, to pick out tasks that the team can complete, and to have a goal to keep everyone on the same page. But the plan doesn't need to have every tiny little detail planned out for every person on the team. This becomes too restrictive and puts too much pressure on the individual each time. Everyone can leave the meeting with an idea of what should happen next and then they can work on getting all the items completed on time.

The idea of Scrum is a process framework that is aimed at helping a company or a team solves some complex problems. These complex problems often need more of an empirical process or the idea of learning by doing. These processes can be hard to plan, so you are never going to come up with the perfect plan when you get started.

It is much better to focus your attention on the outcomes and then get going with the Scrum process!

Chapter 10: Doing a Sprint Review

The next step that you need to focus on during the process of Scrum is the Sprint review. Remember that these reviews are not considered the same thing as a retrospective. A sprint review is all about showing off the hard work of everyone who was on the team. This includes the product owner, the developers, and the designers. These do not need to be in depth or take a lot of time and most companies choose to keep them pretty casual.

During the review, the team members are going to gather around in order to describe all of the work that they have been able to do for the iteration. This is the perfect time for everyone to ask questions, try out some of the new features that were added during that iteration, and give some feedback. While there are some companies that think this is a waste of their time and try to leave it out of the Scrum process, it is definitely something that needs to be done because sharing success can be a great way to build up a team that is agile.

Before we get too far into the sprint review though, it is important to take a look at the definition of "done" in Scrum. This is going to vary from one team to the next and may even change based on the type of project that is being completed. Let's take a look at what this can mean and why it is so important to the review process.

Defining "Done"

Whether you use Jira or another software to help get the process of Scrum done, there is nothing that is more satisfying than being able to move a task from code review over to done. This is a great way to feel more accomplished as a team and to feel like the work you have done throughout the last sprint is finally done and over with. Being able to cross the finish line and get all of that work finished is going to require some good planning, focused execution, and a good definition of what done means.

Most of this work is going to occur during the sprint planning phase, but to make sure that you have a good sprint and a successful sprint review, most teams are going to need to do a bit more than just plan. They must take the time to create a culture that is clear on how to deliver the finished work, as well as a good definition of what they consider done with each work item.

Effective teams are able to bring clear processes and development culture to all of the work items they complete. Some of the questions that you may want to ask to assess your process and to make sure that it works in an optimal way for your team includes:

- Are all the user stories defined well and clearly by the product owner, the engineering team, and the designer before implementing?

- Does everyone understand and follow the values and culture of the engineering team?

- Are there some clear requirements and definitions around code review, continuous integration, and automated testing to help encourage agile development that is sustainable?

- After your team has completed a story, are there a lot of bugs that show up? In other words, does "done" really mean that the project is "done"?

The culture of the team when it comes to completion and quality needs to be above the user story, the work item, and the bug. This culture is going to be reflective of how the team approaches and delivers software.

A clear definition of done can help the team focus on what their end goal is for each of the items they must complete. When the product owner starts to add in more work to the backlog, defining what is known as the acceptance criteria is going to be a key part of how the product owner does this. As they add in the items, they will think about the question "What does it mean for this user story to be complete?" Testing notes and acceptance criteria can help you to figure out the done point for that user story. But what are these two items?

Acceptance criteria: These are the metrics that the product owner is going to use in order to confirm that the story has been implemented in a way that meets their satisfaction.

Testing notes: These are going to be short and focused guidance that comes from the team in charge of quality assistance. They are there to help the development engineer to write better automated tests and feature code.

Having these well-defined issues in the implementation ensures that everyone is going to be successful. You just need to be on the same page with each other. When there is a clear definition of what done means from the very beginning, everyone knows when the sprint is complete and when it is time to celebrate their hard work.

Celebrate the Team

Once the team has determined that their sprint is done, it is time to celebrate the team and all of the work that they completed. Sprint reviews are a great time to celebrate the accomplishments of the team along with the individual accomplishments that each member did during that iteration. You can choose the best time to host them, though at the end of the week seems to work well to lighten up the mood and to celebrate a hard week of work.

Remember that when we talk about a sprint review, we are not talking about a retrospective, so make sure that you do the sprint review in between the end of the iteration and the retrospective. External participants can also come and join, but for the most part, the product owner, the Scrum Master, and everyone on the development team will come and that is plenty. These meetings will usually take less than an hour because you don't want to take up too much time doing this and ruin productivity.

You will find that celebrating the team, as well as the individual accomplishments of its members can be a great way to protect the morale and the health of the team. These are about team building and it is not about an exam or about being adversarial. If there were problems along the way or any issues that need to be solved, save those for the retrospective later on. This is a time for everyone to feel good about their contributions and the fact that they got the sprint done.

It is important that this stage is one that is a very positive activity for everyone on the team. If you find that this isn't turning out to be a positive activity, it could be a sign that there are some problems such as:

- The team is taking on too much work during their sprints and they are not able to get it all done during the iteration. If this happens just once, it's not a big deal and they can finish the work in the next sprint. But if this is happening on a regular basis, it can be a killer for the group morale and the product owner needs to step in and suggest some changes.

- The team is struggling with the technical debt that is already present in the business.

- Features are not being developed sustainably to ensure that new bugs aren't being introduced into the codebase.
- The development practices of the team aren't as developed as they should be. This is something that the team can work on and maybe should be the focus of a short sprint before moving on.

- The product owner decides to change priorities in the middle of a sprint. This brings in scope creep to the team and can really sideline them. The product manager needs to rank all of the items before the sprint starts and if they do change them, it needs to be absolutely necessary.

One thing to note here is that on occasion, every team is going to run into an iteration that is a challenge for them. If this does happen on occasion, then stop and take the time to understand why an iteration changes in the team's retrospective and then work on addressing any issues when you enter into the next sprint.

Reach Across Geographies

Companies that have their team distributed through different areas are going to end up with some special challenges when it comes to scaling their agile ceremonies across these different areas. Sprint reviews are no exception when it comes to these challenges. There are different ways that you can address this problem and hope that it will get a little bit better for you.

One method that has been successful for a lot of companies is for each team to create an informal video that is about five minutes long or so, and then share them on a shared page so the entire team can see from wherever they are. Then the other teams can take some time to view the videos, leave questions and suggestions, and so on at a time that works the best for them.

These informal videos are great because they ensure that everyone on the team is kept as up-to-date as possible on the progress of development, even if there are time differences or other issues that are in the way. Seeing a feature demo first hand by the developer can do wonders for strengthening the whole team in two ways including:

Product understanding: With this method, the entire team is able to hear the intention, rationale, and implementation of the feature. This can make it easier for everyone on the team to understand the entirety of the product.

Team building: These videos do a great job of creating some more personal connections across the team. Each of the members gets to see who is behind all of the aspects of the product. The bridges that are created with this practice can make the individual teams tighter, more cohesive, and more effective regardless of where they are living and working.

For teams that are pretty new to the idea of a sprint review, there is sometimes a temptation to get rid of these reviews or to combine them with the retrospective. But the review needs to be its own ceremony. Take the time to enjoy all the hard work that the team has been able to do together. This does wonders when it comes to building up motivation and the morale of the team and will actually make them more productive and easier to work with in the future.

Chapter 11: The Importance of a Sprint Retrospective

The final step that comes with working on a sprint is for the whole team to perform a sprint retrospective. This is a time when the whole team comes together and reflects on what went right with the sprint, what can be improved, and anything else that needs to be mentioned when it comes to working on the next sprint.

The agile manifesto made it clear that this retrospective was necessary. In order to use the agile values the right way, any team that used it needs to meet on a regular basis in order to check in and make the necessary adjustments. Most commonly, the development team needs to apply this principle simply by hosting meetings to do this on a regular basis.

Sometimes, it can seem a bit crazy to take the time to go over the last sprint before you can go through the next one. These sprints are so short that it may feel like a better option to be able to just move on to the next sprint and maybe check in once or twice a year. The reason that a team should get excited about these retrospectives is that this is how the idea of agile can really come into place. Think about the following values that come with agile:

- Individuals and interactions over any tools and processes.
- Responding to change over following a set plan.

At face value, these two are basically what the retrospective is all about. It is about working with real people in order to make any improvements and changes that are necessary. Very few things are going to help reinforce these principles in a better way. Now that we have a better idea about why these retrospectives are so important, let's take a look at how to host one of these meetings with your team at the end of every sprint.

The Meeting

These retrospectives can be a great way for your whole team to do an evaluation of itself and then it will go through and create a plan to address any areas that they need to improve in the future. The whole meeting is going to embrace the idea of trying to improve all the time. Many times, complacency is going to be the end of a particular team or business. They get into the idea that they are doing things well enough and they should just leave it there. But if you want to keep your business moving forward and the team wants to be as productive and efficient as possible, then this is not the mindset to have. To do this, the retrospective is going to step the team out of its work cycle so they can reflect a bit more on the past. The whole purpose of this meeting is to do the following:

- The team is going to take a look at the last work item, iteration, or sprint and see how it went. They want to specifically take a look at the tools, the processes, and the team dynamic and discuss if there is anything that needs improvement.

- They will articulate and then stack rank items that ended up doing well for them. They can also do the same thing with some of the items that didn't do as well for them.

- The team can then create, as well as implement a plan that they want to follow that improves the way that the team does its work together.

This retrospective is going to provide a very safe place for the members of the team to focus on adaptation and introspection. For this meeting to be successful, the atmosphere there needs to be supportive and will encourage (without forcing) all the team members to contribute as much as possible.

While there may be a few negative things that get discussed during this meeting, this retrospective needs to be an experience that is energizing and positive for the whole team. It can help when team members share feedback, learn how to let go of some of their frustrations, and then work together to figure out the right solutions.

If there are any facilitators that come with this meeting, they can gain a great understanding of how the team works together and what challenges and successes they experienced in the last sprint. A good retrospective is going to result in a list of improvements that team members take ownership of and work towards in their future sprints.

How to Do the First Retrospective

While it can be beneficial for the team to determine their own retrospective and vary the format a bit, there are certain aspects like the general format, attendees, and timing that should remain constant and consistent for each of these meetings to make things easier.

First, we are going to look at the end. For the team that is working with a two-week sprint, the retrospective needs to be done at the very end of every sprint. For teams that do these for a month or longer, then you need to have this kind of meeting at least once a month. During this time, it is also a good idea to engage members of the broader leadership after major initiatives are rolled out. But be careful to not focus energy and attention on what was delivered but rather on how the team was able to get things done by working together.

These meetings take somewhere between 30 to 60 minutes, depending on the length of the sprint and how much was covered during that time period.

The Who

Every member who worked on the Scrum team needs to attend this meeting and it may be helpful to bring in a facilitator. This is an individual that can be helpful during the first meeting to ensure that everyone is able to express their feelings without any issues arising. The first retrospective can sometimes be tough because there are likely to be a lot of issues that should be discussed between the team and this can make tempers rise a bit. A facilitator can help to remind everyone that this is a place for sharing and can lead them to think clearly when making new solutions.

Of course, the facilitator can be anyone you would like. Sometimes the team will bring in someone completely new, but often the Scrum Master or the Product owner will be able to handle this. This individual can even be someone from the team if wanted. During this meeting, you may also want to bring in people from marketing, the design team, or anyone else who contributed during that particular sprint.

The what

There are different ways that you can mix up this meeting, but you need to go with the one that works the best for the team you are working on now. Below, we are going to have a basic template that you can use during this meeting. This is a good one to work with during your first retrospective, but you can certainly change it up and make it work the way that works the best for your team and the sprint that you just completed. The basic template that you can bring to this meeting includes:

- Create a short list of all the things that went well and then make a second list of what can be improved. You can have everyone write out a short list on their own or bring out the marker and write out suggestions for these lists on the board. Make the list in any method that you want as long as you get the initial feedback from the whole team. Make sure that in the end, it is written down the proper way to ensure that the team members are able to reference it down the road if needed.

- Prioritize this list by importance: No person is able to do this on their own. Make sure that the whole team is prioritizing this list based on the way that they want it to. You may find that there are some themes that are common, which means that you are able to group these together to save some time.
- Discuss some tactics to help improve the top two items on the room for improvement list. You want to go through this and focus on outcomes, rather than the past, on people, and on actions.
- Create an action plan: By the end of this meeting, the team should have a clear idea of the actionable ideas that they want to follow along with due dates, clear owners, and more. The team should have some great ways to address the areas of improvement.

Be disciplined as a team to execute the last option. Nothing is more frustrating than the team working hard and then finds that every time they get back to this meeting that you are dealing with the same roadblocks again. Avoid stagnation, as well as some frustration by making sure that each member of the team is able to walk away with a clear idea of the steps they will take. Each action item that was identified in the beginning needs to have its own owner to follow through to completion.

Taking the time to standardize the retrospective that you are working on and any of them that come up in the future is a great way to create consistency and to build up trust through the team over time. But there are sometimes a few tweaks that a facilitator may try to use that can provide more insights, encourages new team members to participate some more, or at least keeps the meetings interesting. Some of the ways that you can mix up these meetings a little bit include:

Bring in a new facilitator to help out

Typically, these meetings are going to be run by either the product owner or the Scrum Master. But you may find that bringing in someone new to lead the next one can be fun. You may find that the dynamics of the team shift in a way that is positive because there is someone who doesn't have any skin in the game that leads the discussion. In addition, this strategy can allow someone else who is in the company to observe how these teams work and they may be able to implement them better in their own department.

Vary the list prompts

At the end of the day, this meeting is meant to figure out what works and what doesn't among the team. But getting to this may get boring over some time. You may want to consider some of these different prompts to make things easier at the next meeting:

- Start, stop, and continue: During this one, you can first focus on what the team can start doing, then on what the team should stop doing, and then on what the team can continue doing. Focus on ways to discontinue items that are in the stop column.
- More/less: With this one, you can first focus on what the team should do more of and then focus on what the team can do less of. Then, based on the answers that the team provides, you can create a plan that talks about how to tackle the items that are on the "do less" list.

- Glad, sad, mad: Now you can discuss what first made the team glad, and then what made the team sad, and then what made the team mad. You want to spend your time more on what made the team mad and sad and how you can improve it. Over time, you want to see those two lists go down while the glad list starts to go up.

Changing up the list prompts can go a long way to ensuring that everyone will talk about what is going on with the team and puts everyone on the same page when everything is done. Make sure that you mix it up on occasion or at least find a method that seems to work the best for your team.

Engage the leadership some more

After a big project is completed and has rolled out, it may be a good idea to schedule an hour with someone who is in the leadership team and then focus on the different ways that the team worked together. You want to make sure that the leadership of the company is on your side during this process and that they know what is going on as well. They may soon like what they hear and want to implement this same process throughout other parts of the company after they see how well it works. Keeping them in the loop and up to date on what is going on can be the best way to make this happen.

In most instances, you need to do this retrospective at the end of your sprint. Since most sprints are going to last about two weeks, this ensures that the team is getting together and discussing any changes that are needed on a regular basis. If you do a longer sprint, you will need to decide how often this needs to occur. If the sprint is three to four weeks, it is probably fine to wait until the end of the sprint to do the meeting, especially if you only do sprints this long for a short amount of time. But if the sprint is longer, it may be a better idea to do a few of these to ensure that any issues are addressed right away and fixed before they become major issues down the road.

There are so many benefits when it comes to doing this retrospective meeting. It is sometimes one that teams will want to bleed together with the review or even one that they want to just skip over in favor of getting other work done, but it is important to spend time on this part, just like you do with any of the other meetings during the sprint.

Spending time on this meeting is going to ensure that the team is able to work well together into the future. It helps everyone on the team discuss what they think went well with their project, what they think may need some improvements and more. The team can then take this information and use it to help them make decisions in the future. Overall, if this meeting is handled properly, it can make it easier for the team to learn how to work together effectively and see the best results.

Chapter 12: How to Use the Burndown Charts in Scrum

A burndown chart is going to show how much work the team has been able to complete during an epic or a sprint, along with the total amount of work that still needs to be down. These burndown charts are then used to help predict the likelihood that the team is actually going to be able to finish the work based on the timeline they assigned for the sprint. This chart is also a great way to ensure that no scope creep starts to get into the project.

These burndown charts are very useful because they can provide a lot of insight into how the team works together. For example:

- If you start to notice that the team is consistently finishing their work earlier than the sprint, this may be a sign that they aren't taking on enough work during their sprint planning session.

- If they consistently miss their forecast and can't get the committed work done in time, this is often a sign that your team is taking on too much work during each sprint.

- If you take a look at the burndown chart and notice that there is a large drop during the sprint, this is a sign that the items or the work are not estimated properly or they are not broken down in the proper manner.

One of the first things that you need to do when working on your burndown charts is set up an estimation statistic. This is a unit of measurement that your team is going to use to help them measure and estimate the work that needs to be done. With most Scrum software, you are able to measure out the work with the help of hours, story points, or you can choose your own statistics to put in at this place.

This estimation statistic can be very important because it is used to help calculate the velocity of the team. During each of the sprints that you work on, the velocity is going to be the sum of your estimation statistics for all of the completed stories. If your team remains pretty consistent with its velocity, it becomes infinitely easier to determine the amount of work that they can handle during each sprint and this can be very helpful when you work on sprint planning.

Setting the estimation statistic is pretty easy. You need to navigate to the board or the backlog and then select on more and then board settings. From here, you should click on the Estimation tab. Now we are at the question, which estimation statistic should we use? Traditionally, software teams are going to estimate their work based on a time format, relying on days, weeks, and months. However, there are many teams who use agile that have moved over to story points. If you are unsure about which one to use and you are using the agile system, it is best to stick with story points.

Now it is it time to estimate your issues. In agile, estimation is going to refer to measuring the size of the team's backlog or the amount of work that the team needs to complete. B tracking is going to refer to using those estimates to ensure that the work can be done on time. To help you set an estimation for one of your issues, you need to first be inside your Scrum project. From there, you can select an issue either through the backlog or on the board. In the issue details, you will want to click on the Estimate field. Then enter in the estimation that you want to use for that issue.

It is possible to go through and change an estimation after you have entered it into the system, but remember that if you change this value once the sprint has officially started, it is going to show up like a scope change in your burndown chart. If you find that it is hard to estimate some of the issues, this is normal so don't worry! Just try to do your best and discuss the best possible estimations with your team.

Next, you can work on tracking the progress of your team with a burndown chart. This is a report that will show the work that the team has been able to do in the sprint and we talked about it a bit before. This is definitely something that you should pay attention to. Having this information makes it much easier for you to make sound decisions on future sprints and can ensure that the work for that current sprint will be done on time. Any time that you would like to view the burndown chart for that project, you simply need to use the following steps to bring it up:

- Navigate over to your current Scrum project.

- Select the Backlog or Active Sprint
- Click on Reports. From there you should be able to click on Burndown Chart.

There are a few different parts that are going to be present on this chart. First, there is the estimation statistic. This is the vertical axis which is going to show you an estimation of any statistic that you selected and want to look at. Then there are the remaining values. This is a red line on the chart that can show the total amount of work that is left inside that particular sprint according to the estimates that your team gives.

And the third part of a traditional burndown chart is the guideline. This is going to be a grey line that shows a good approximation of where the team should be, with the assumption that linear progression is happening. If you see that the red line is below this grey line, this is a sign that the team is right on track on getting all the work done by the time the sprint ends. This isn't foolproof though and if you know one part will take a bit longer than others, it might be perfectly fine if the red line goes above the grey one for a little bit.

We can also work with an epic burndown chart in this Framework. This kind of chart is a report that will show you how your team is progressing against the work for an epic. This one has had optimization for Scrum Teams who work in sprints and can make the process of tracking much easier. Some of the ways that you are able to use this kind of burndown chart include:

- To check how quickly the team is able to work through the epic.

- See how any work has been added and removed through that sprint and see how it affects the overall progress of your team.

- Predict the number of sprints that it takes to complete the work for that epic. This is going to be based on some past sprints and on changes that may come up during the sprint.

Finding the epic burndown chart is pretty easy to work with. You just need to navigate to the main page of your Scrum project and then select on Active Sprint or Backlog. Click on Reports and then on Epic Burndown. From here, you will select an epic that you want to use from the drop-down box. You can choose from any of the epics that are in projects and are configured to the board using the filter. There are a few main parts that you should understand when it comes to using an epic burndown chart and these include:

- The epic menu: This is going to help you select which of the epics you want to view data for.

- Work added: This is going to be the darker blue segment that shows the amount of work that is added to the sprint during each of the sprints. Often this is done in story points but you can use another measurement option if you would like.

- Work remaining: This is going to be the lighter blue segment that shows you how much work is left in the epic.

- Work completed: This is the green segment of the chart that will show you how much work is completed for that epic during each of the sprints the team does.

- Projected completion: This is the report that is going to project how many sprints the team thinks it will take for them to complete the epic. This number needs to be based on the current velocity of the team to make sure that it is accurate.

These are the two main types of burndown charts that you are able to work with. You may find that working with the Release burndown chart can be nice as well. Many teams like to add this to their plan to ensure that they are on track on getting things done.

It is going to be based on the items that the team has to do, the amount that they are currently working on, and the amount that they have completed. And it can be updated for each sprint to make sure that everyone is on the same page throughout. Team members can always go take a look at the burndown chart to figure out where they are during the sprint and how much still needs to be done with that sprint. Make sure to implement this into your Scrum project and have team members get into the habit of using this form of tracking tool to ensure they are always on the same page and getting all the work done during each of the sprints.

Chapter 13: The Important Role of the Scrum Master

One of the important roles that we need to discuss a bit in this guidebook is that of the Scrum Master. This individual is a servant leader for the Scrum Team. They are responsible for promotion and supporting Scrum. They are able to do this by helping everyone on the team understand what Scrum is, the practices, the rules, and the values.

They are basically the facilitators of the Scrum, a lightweight and agile framework that is going to focus on time-boxed iterations that are known as sprints. As the facilitators, these masters are going to be similar to the coaches for the rest of the team. They are committed to the basic foundations of Scrum, but they will remain flexible and open to opportunities for their whole team to do well and improve the workflow.

In an ideal world, the team is able to manage their own processes and their own tools. However, there are many teams that make the big leap over to the Agile system and then rely on the Scrum Master as the owner of this process. It is sometimes going to take some time before the authority and responsibility start to diffuse over to the team, and in the meantime, it is fine to let the Scrum Master be a kind of leader, as long as it doesn't detract from the hard work that the team does.

There are a few responsibilities that the Scrum Master is supposed to follow according to the official Scrum Guide. Some of the most common ones (though certainly not an exhaustive list) includes:

- Standups: The Scrum Master is going to facilitate the daily standups for the daily scrum, any time that it is needed.

- Iteration/sprint planning meetings: They will be there during the meetings and can watch the different goals of the team. They aren't there to dictate exactly what happens, but they may watch out that no scope cream or over-committing occurs so that the task can actually be completed. They can also aid in some of the estimations for the sprints and in creating sub-tasks.

- Sprint review: They are going to spend some time participating in the sprint reviews done. They can also capture some of the feedback in case there are questions later on.

- Retrospectives: These are so important when it comes to finishing up a project and the Scrum Master can attend these and provide some valuable insight as well. They will take a look at some areas for improvement and can write down any action items that should be included in future sprints.

- Board administration: The Scrum Master can work as an administrator of the scrum board. This ensures that the cards are always up to date and the scrum tool, the Jira software is working the way that it should.

- One on ones: There are times when the Scrum Master may need to meet with some of the team members individually. This can be used to deal with any disagreements inside the team about work styles and processes. While this is something that some teams decide to go aghast because they believe that this will take away from the team mindset, sometimes this is a preferable way to deal with issues.

- Internal consulting: Scrum Masters should be prepared to do any consulting with team members, as well as with other internal stakeholders on the best methods for working with the scrum team.

- Reporting: A regular analysis of the burndown charts and other planning tools can be useful for the Scrum Master to get down to help report what has happened with the team during each sprint.

- Blockers: This individual can aid the team by getting rid of any types of external blockers, as well as managing internal roadblocks through a process or workflow improvements. This ensures that there aren't a lot of unnecessary regulations, noise, and distractions that keep the team from getting their work done.

- Busy work: If there is some reason that the team isn't getting things done and being productive, then this is a problem the Scrum Master needs to fix. This could be things such as adjusting the thermostat, moving desks around, fixing computers when they are broken, finding ways to get rid of distractions, and so much more. As a Scrum Master, the individual should become comfortable doing just about anything that they need to ensure that their team can concentrate and get their work done.

The next question is whether or not a team really needs to work with a Scrum Master. This is going to depend on your team and on your process. Many teams find that when they are starting out, it is really helpful to have someone in the role who has worked with Scrum before and can help lead and direct the team on how they can get things done. Later on, the team may decide that they have enough confidence to do the work on their own. This is why many times, the Scrum Master is going to be hired more as a consultant, rather than as a full-time employee.

Of course, every Scrum team is going to be a bit different. Sometimes a more experienced team is able to handle the responsibilities that this individual would take all on their own and they will just share the management and leadership role. Others find that having a dedicated person to do this job works better for them when it comes to getting it done.

If you do decide to add in a Scrum Master, make sure that it is a dedicated person who knows Scrum and will have this as their main job. There is sometimes a misunderstanding of the Scrum Masters role and an existing manager may think that it is their role. If a manager is willing to go through the training and learn how to use this Framework, it is fine to have them take this position. But they should not automatically move into that position simply because they manage a particular team in the past or because of the department that they manage at the time.

A Scrum Master can be a great addition to the team. While you may decide to let the team do the work and report to the product owner, it can be really helpful to deal with a Scrum Master to make things easier. These individuals are there to keep the team in order, to answer questions, to keep the workflow going, and to help share their experience with the Scrum process to a team that may not have any knowledge of it to start with.

Chapter 14: The Flow of the Scrum Framework

While the Scrum Framework is meant to make things easier and to ensure that everyone has a job to do and is on the same page when you first get started on it, there are a lot of different things going on and it can be hard for team members to keep track of everything. Even some of the terms, in the beginning, can be overwhelming. The important thing to remember and that can help you keep things in line when you first get started, is that all Scrum Projects have five essential activities that can ensure that your product development process goes well.

Being able to use each of these processes will enhance the performance of the process, and can even help your team be more efficient from the beginning, all the way to the end of the project. These five steps are often called the Scrum Process Flow. The five parts that you need to complete the scrum process flow include:

Sprint

This is used by the scrum team. A sprint is a short development period of time where the team is going to create product functionality. These sprints are never going to last very long, often between one to four weeks depending on what goals you are trying to reach. Sometimes you may get the process done in one day. These sprints are going to have a short development cycle and you should never let it take over 4 weeks. The planned economic value is going to be determined based on how long the sprint is, so if it takes longer than originally thought, then that means more money spent.

Sprint planning

At the beginning of a sprint, the scrum team needs to get together and have a meeting. This is the meeting where the team is going to decide and then commit to their goal for that sprint. The product owner needs to be there as well, presenting the product backlog, explaining the tasks, and discussing with the team the tasks they would like to work on.

During this planning session, the team needs to figure out what requirements they will use to help them support the goal and what they are going to need during the sprint. The team can then identify the individual tasks that it will make for them to reach their goals.

Daily Scrum

In addition to the scrum planning meeting that we talked about above, it is also important for the team to meet on a regular basis to discuss the goals, check what has gotten done, and more. The meeting should happen each day for about fifteen minutes and should include the Scrum Master along with the Scrum Team. During this meeting, the team needs to spend time coordinating their priorities. They will talk about what needs to get done first during the day, what they got done on the previous day and any of the roadblocks that they ran into when they are doing work that day.

This is a very important part of the Scrum Framework. Some may worry that this is going to be a waste of their time, but in reality, it is going to make a big difference in how effective the team can be overall. It can help to streamline the process and can prevent any issues popping up that the team isn't really prepared for.

Sprint review

This is a meeting that the product owner will need to introduce. It will also occur at the end of each sprint. During this meeting, the scrum team is going to show off the working product's functionality that they were able to complete during the previous sprint. The team is meant to showcase all the work that they were able to complete during that sprint, and if everything went well, they should have something to show the product owner. The product doesn't have to be completely done, but it needs to be at a good point to try out and show off.

During this meeting, the product owner is going to determine whether that whole sprint backlog has been covered or not. In most cases, if the team did the work that they were supposed to, the product owner will sign off on the work and will let them work on the next sprint. If the team didn't do the job right though, it is possible that something could be put back into the backlog so that it is corrected before moving on.

Sprint retrospective

Similar to what happens with the sprint review, the team needs to do a sprint retrospective before moving on to the next step. This one is not going to be led by the product owner, but should be done by the team instead and the product master can be there as well.

During this time, the team needs to discuss the last sprint. They can discuss what went well, what they would like to see change, and the best ways to make those changes. And if there are any issues with the team working efficiently together, they can discuss ways to fix this as well. It is important that everyone speak up about any issues they experienced. Failure to do this early on can result in more problems down the road, which can be detrimental to how well the project will work later on.

All of these steps are important and they all need to happen during each of the sprints that occur with your project. They help you to know which steps and tasks need to be completed, help you to review what is going on each day and what you should work on next, can ensure that you see results at the end of the sprint, and can ensure that the following sprints work out well. Make sure that your team is aware of these different steps and that each step is followed during every sprint to improve efficiency, to keep everyone on the same page, and to ensure the work gets done.

Chapter 15: The Different Stages of a Successful Sprint

Putting a group of people together so that they can accomplish a task as complicated as Scrum can be hard. It is necessary to make sure that everyone always works towards a common goal and it will require a specific process that is known as the Group Development Process.

This process is a five-step program that can be implemented to help your team be as successful as possible. The first four stages that we will talk about known as forming, storming, norming, and performing were developed in 1965 by Bruce Tuckman. According to Tuckman, these were the stages that were necessary for the Scrum team to grow and using this kind of process can make it easier for the team to face challenges, tackle any problems that come up, plan out work, find solutions, and deliver the best results that they can.

Later on, Tuckman decided to add in the 5th stage known as Adjourning. And when it comes to Agile software development, many teams are going to show a behavior that is known as swarming. This is a performance where the team comes together, collaborates, and then focuses their energy on solving a singular problem.

When you use this Group Development Process, it can lead to a mature and efficient team. It is necessary to remember that sometimes a process like this one is going to take you some time. One issue that can come with this is that many companies want to see immediate results and they want to jump right into a task right away, without thinking about team building or some of the other things that can make the team more efficient. When you use this development process, it leads to some positive impacts and can ensure better success.

These five stages can be important to ensuring that your sprints are always successful, no matter what the team is working on. The five stages that your team needs to focus on include:

Forming stage

It is very important for the team to start off as successfully as possible. This stage is going to be a good one for the team members to get to know one another. They should find out what they have in common, what they have as differences, and how they can learn from one another. This is a great time for the team to connect in the ways that are necessary for them to work together efficiently and seamlessly.

If you do skip this step, it is hard for the team to move through some of the other steps of this process. You want your team to connect with each other and be ready to work together as much as possible.

A good way to ensure that your team members are able to connect with each other during this forming stage is to do a fun icebreaker.

You can make this as simple or as complex as you would like. You can have them share personal information, do a fun game, or anything else that you think will help the team members get to know each other better, especially if they have never worked together before.

Also, this is the stage where the team members are going to look more at a group leader for some direction and guidance. The members are searching for acceptance in the group and they want that group to feel like they are in a safe space. They want to keep things simple, without controversy, which means that many serious feelings and topics will be avoided at this time. Just let them get to know each other and have a team leader present to help lead the group and keep everything in order, but some of the deeper issues can come into play a little later on.

Storming stage

The next stage is going to be the storming stage. This is the stage where many conflicts, as well as competition, can occur. The fear of exposure and the fear of failure can show up here. Members are going to question which of them is the one in charge, who is going to be responsible for each part, what the rules are, and what the criteria for any evaluations are going to be, and even the reward system that is in place.

There are times when you will see some behavioral changes in attitudes based on competition and the issues that it presents. Some team members may ally together, especially if they knew each other before this process. Some members may start to feel more comfortable speaking up in front of others and then some members want to stay silent. If this is not handled properly, it is possible for your Scrum team to start splintering up and stop acting as a team, which can be detrimental to the success that you want.

The best way for you to solve any conflicts that arise is through a collaborative and problem solving based approach. This is the only way that your team is going to unify and start working together. The only reason for you to decide to skip this test is if the team you choose for the Scrum Framework has been established and has worked together for some time. They are most likely familiar with the working style of all the members and you can skip on to the next step to save some time.

Norming stage

Now it is time to talk about the norming stage. This is the stage that is all about cohesion within the group. It is important for every member to acknowledge the contributions of each other, the community building of each member, and their attempt to solve any group issues. Team members need to have some willingness to change their previous opinions and ideas when they see facts from other team members. This needs to go along with asking questions for each other.

During this stage, the team needs to realize that the leadership will be shared between all of them and that there is no need for cliques or for an official leader. Having all of the members get to know each other and learn how to identify with each other can be so important to strengthening trust and this helps the team to grow and become more efficient.

During the Scrum process, you want to make sure that the team is able to work together pretty well. You want them to work together, take leadership for the work that they want to do, bounce ideas off each other, share the work, and so much more. This is the stage where you ensure that the team is set up with all of the tools that they need to get this done.

Performing stage

This is a stage that can be hard for some groups to reach. But if your team is able to reach this point, it means that they are tight-knit and trust each other and they are ready to perform the Scrum tasks efficiently. Team members in this stage are able to work on the project at hand, either on their own, in subgroups, or as a whole and be productive in equal parts. The people on the team are able to change their roles and make any adjustments that they need depending on what the team needs to have done. Group loyalty and morale is high and they can work well to get any project done that is needed.

Adjourning stage

Remember in the beginning that we talked about how this stage wasn't really part of the original process and it was actually added in quite a bit later. But just because it was added later doesn't mean it isn't a step that you need to have there. When your team reaches this point, it is likely that the team has fulfilled the vision of the project. While the technical sides of things are completed, the team needs to go through and check in with things on a more personal level before moving on.

The team needs to take this time to reflect on how well they were able to work together as a team and honestly talk about what improvements they could make together. The team can also work here to recognize any achievements that were made, as a group or individually. The team spent a lot of time working on an intense project together and this time can help them to wrap up the process, both on the technical level as well as a personal level, can help everyone feel like they finished without any loose strings to tie up.

Sometimes, it is hard for a team to follow all these stages. You might have someone on the team who is really stubborn and there are times when certain types of people just don't even up working well together. To ensure that the team that is implementing Scrum is able to reach its best potential, they must all be flexible enough to accept when it is time to ask for help. The good news is that there are a few steps that the group can take to help them develop properly through all the different stages and these include:

1. The group needs to make sure that they are changing up the group facilitator responsibility. If one person starts to take over the lead all the time, it can shift the dynamics away from what you want with the team and can make issues with competition and more show up. Everyone on the team needs to have a chance to be the one in charge. This helps to ensure that everyone feels equal and included.

2. The mission and the purpose of the group need to be clear to everyone in the team. And the mission should be something that they all look over often, just in case someone forgets or things start to change for some reason. It is possible that as you go through the process, the mission is going to change depending on how a sprint goes and even based on the feedback that a customer provides. Keeping the statement updated can ensure that all members of the team are able to stay on task.

3. Rules are important to the team and you need to establish them early on and then monitor them through the whole process. Having these rules may seem unnecessary, but they help all the team members know where things stand and what they should be doing if a rule is in question or broken during a sprint.

4. The group needs to remember that conflict can actually be a very positive thing and it is actually very normal. In some cases, it can be necessary to help the team develop. One member may go against another when it comes to completing a task. Since these two members disagree, they may come up with a third method that is more efficient for completing the task. They must be willing to work together and not just get stuck in a fight, but a bit of conflict is never a bad thing.

5. The group needs to remember that listening can be just as important as talking. Having one person who just speaks over all the other members is never productive and it can often make the group feel upset or resentful. If everyone remembers that they should take time to listen, then it allows others to have a chance to talk as well.

6. Each session with the team needs to end with some constructive criticism and never with harsh advice. It is important to lift each other up and be helpful with each other, instead of trying to put each other down.

7. Everyone needs to be a part of doing the work. No person should ever end up doing all the work. This makes that person resentful to doing the work and there is no way that they can get things done in time on their own. Plus, the other team members will never feel a sense of pride in the work that they are doing. Each person on the team should be willing to pull their own weight. If one refuses to do it, then it may be time to consider restructuring the team a bit.

The Scrum team is an integral part of the whole process. Yes, there are a few other individuals who are there to help keep things organized, to set the rules, and to make sure that things get done. But the team is the main part that actually does the work and moves the product development process forward. Ensuring that they are able to work well together and get through each of their sprints successfully can go a long way in how successful this framework will turn out.

Chapter 16: How to Scale Scrum

Scrum was a framework that was originally introduced as a method that should only be used for some smaller projects. Many believed for a long time that it was only good for these smaller projects, without realizing that it was possible to take this framework and scale it to some bigger projects as well. So, how can you even take this framework and scale it? Is it actually possible? This chapter is going to take a look at how you can consider scaling Scrum to make it work on any size of the project that you would like.

Ideally, your Scrum team is going to stay somewhere between six and ten members. However, if you do run into an issue where you need more than ten people, this is still possible with this framework. You would form more than one team, rather than sticking all of them together when the members get to more than ten. Doing this can be a great option when it comes to larger projects, but you will find that it still requires a lot of open communication and synchronization because the different teams need to work together, as well as in their own group.

When you separate your members out into different teams, they will each have a job to do. Each team needs to pick their own representative who is then responsible for meeting with the other representatives. These individuals are going to update each other about the progress they are making, the different challenges that they are facing, and then they will make plans to coordinate their activities. How often these meetings occur will be determined by the size of the project, how complex this particular project is going to be, how dependent the different teams are on each other, and the recommendations that the Scrum Guidance Body give.

If you do end up in a situation where you need to divide up your groups into different teams and they need to have representatives that meet and discuss what each group is doing, you may be wondering how you would get these meetings to work exactly? It is recommended that the teams have face to face communication, meaning that they meet together in the same room, if possible. Now, there are times when this isn't possible.

If your company is large and your two teams work in different parts of the country and in different time zones, then doing this can be pretty hard. These representatives need to meet on a pretty regular basis and if they are far apart from each other, it doesn't make sense time wise and with money to have them get together like this. If this is a problem for your teams, then working with video conference calls and social media can work well too.

During these meetings, the Chief Scrum Master will run the show and this individual will be assisted by the representatives for each team including the Scrum Master for the individual teams. For projects that are really large which have a ton of different teams, you may need to have a lot of these meetings. And because it is hard for you to get everyone together at the same time in some instances, it is important that all matters that are critical are discussed right at the beginning of any meeting that does take place.

Before the meeting does take place though, the Chief Scrum Master needs to announce the agenda and then send it out to each of the individual teams. These teams need to take the time to look over the agenda. This helps them to get a good idea of what is going to be discussed at the next meeting and then they can also think about what other items should be discussed at this meeting. If there are any risks, changes, and issues that could affect any of the other teams, then this needs to be brought up and discussed during that meeting.

Remember that even if there is a problem that one particular team is facing in this, then it needs to be brought up. Often an issue that seems localized and like it is just affecting one team can end up causing harm to a lot of the other teams as well if it goes without being mentioned. Bringing it up early can ensure that the issue doesn't spread to the other teams and even if it doesn't affect the other teams, they can still provide advice to the individual team to help them get through the challenge.

During these meetings, the individual representatives for each team need to take the time to provide an update to the other teams. When they do talk, there are four guidelines that they can follow to ensure they cover everything important, without wasting a lot of time along the way. The four guidelines that should be followed when providing an update include:

- What work has my team gotten done since we last spoke?
- What will my team work on until the next meeting?

- Is there anything that remains unfinished that the other teams were expecting to be done?
- Will what we're doing affects the other teams?

This provides a good summary of the things that your team is working on, what you are going to do next, and more. This helps the other teams to see where the progress is as well. Take some good notes as you listen to the other teams during this process as well. You may be able to gain some insights and advice that can make the work on your side easier as well.

The most important rule that comes with these meetings is that you must ensure that there is some great coordination that occurs across the different teams. No team should be working on their own or feel like they are lost, forgotten, or confused in the process. If one team gets left out or one team gets too far ahead and abandons the others, then the process of scaling Scrum is never going to work. And since many of the teams are going to depend on each other, at least a little bit, it is best that there is open communication, plenty of meetings to check up on each other, and a general idea that each team is going to do their work and get it done in a timely manner. Doing this is going to ensure that your scaled Scrum project is able to get the best results possible without running into any issues in the meantime.

Chapter 17: A Scrum Tutorial with the Help of Jira Software

Now that we have taken some time to learn a bit more about the Scrum Framework and what it means, it is time to go through and actually complete a project with this tool. This chapter is going to go through the different steps that you can take to help you get started with this kind of project using the Jira Software.

The first step is to create and then log into your account for the Jira Software. Then you can create a project. When you see the prompt to select a project template, make sure that you click on Scrum. If you don't do that, you will end up creating a Kanban project. Once you have been able to create the project, you are going to end up on an empty backlog. This is your Product Backlog and will contain all of the items that could be potential work items for your team during this project.

Next, stay in the Jira Software. We are going to call the work items such as bugs, tasks, and user stories "issues". Creating a few of these user stories just by clicking on the quick create option in the backlog is pretty easy. If you don't have any in mind for this project yet, go ahead and just make up a few to give you an idea of what it takes to make this process work.

Once you have been able to create a few of these user stories (or make a few up to experiment with this system), you can go through and prioritize them in your backlog. Inside the Jira Software, you can rank these stories simply by dragging and then dropping them in the order that you want the stories to be worked on. These are just the starting stories for a project. You are always going to be adding and creating stories throughout the life cycle of your project. This is simply because agility is going to involve continuously learning and adapting.

At this point, it is time to create the first sprint that your team needs to work on in the backlog. Then you can start planning out that sprint. What is a sprint? In Scrum, the team is going to forecast that they can complete a set of work items and user stories during a fixed time period which will be a sprint. In most cases, the sprint is not going to be over four weeks long and the team will be able to determine how long the sprint can be. Two weeks is a good amount of time because the team has time to accomplish some work, but they don't go too long without getting feedback.

From here, you want to hold a sprint planning meeting with the rest of the team. This meeting is like a little ceremony where you set up the entire team with the information that they need to be successful during the rest of the sprint. In this meeting, the team is going to discuss their goals, what work items they want to prioritize, and more.
In addition, during this meeting, the development team will get to work to complete a certain number of stories during the sprint. These stories and the plan that is going to be used to complete them will become the sprint backlog.

After the team has had some time to get together and discuss the plans they want to accomplish during the sprint, it is time to actually get started on the sprint. At this point, make sure to name the sprint to help you keep things organized as you move from one sprint to another. You can do this along with adding the duration (or the start and end dates) of the sprint into Jira. Make sure that these start and end dates will align with the schedule that your team has set out in that planning meeting. Add in the sprint goals which should match up with what the team decided during the meeting.

Once the sprint is started, you will be taken to the Active sprints tab in the project. This is where the team is able to work to pick up items that are in the to-do column and then move them over to the in-progress column. When the project is done, they can move it over to the complete column as well. This is basically going to be the Scrum Board that the team can use to monitor what tasks need to be done, which tasks are being worked on right then, and which tasks have been completed.

As the project progresses and after the sprint has begun, the team needs to meet up daily. Typically meeting in the morning is best before people are tired or have to run out the door to get other things done. This meeting can be short — ten to fifteen minutes is usually plenty to get the work done. Everyone will review the work that is being done and to check if anyone on the team is running into any roadblocks when it comes to completing the sprint tasks.

While this meeting should be kept pretty short, you want to make sure that everyone on the team has time to talk and that it doesn't become controlled by one or two people. Using a timer can be a great way to keep people on track or tossing the ball around. Everyone gets a few minutes to talk then problems can be solved, everyone is on the same page and everyone knows what they need to do to finish the day.

It is also a good idea to check in often with the Burndown Chart during this sprint. In the Jira Software, the chart is going to show the actual, as well as the estimated amount of work that needs to be done on a sprint. This chart is going to be automatically updated through Jira as you complete some of the work items. If you ever need to get in and review this chart, just click on the Reports Tab from the sidebar. Then select on the Burndown Chart from the reports drop-down menu that shows up.

Remember from earlier that the Burndown Chart is going to show both the actual and the estimated amount of work that you need to get done during the sprint. The horizontal x-axis is going to indicate the time and the vertical axis is going to indicate the story points. This is a great tool that lets you see how much time is left in the sprint and the amount of work that the team needs to continue working on. By taking the time to track all the remaining work through the iteration, a team is better able to manage its progress and respond in the proper manner. Some of the patterns that you should be careful about when looking at this chart include:

- The team finishes too early with many of the sprints. This is an issue because it often means that they aren't committing to the right amount of work each sprint. Finishing early on occasion is not a big deal. Finishing early all the time can be a problem.

- The team misses their forecast sprint after sprint. This has the opposite effect and means that the team is trying to take on too much work. Sometimes things happen and the team falls behind, but this should not be a regular occurrence.

- The Burndown line makes a steep drop rather than a gradual burndown because the work wasn't broken into granular pieces.

- The product owners start to change or add to the scope in the middle of the sprint.

At any point, either during or after your sprint, you want to take a look at the Sprint Report to get a good idea of how that sprint is going. The sprint report will include the Burndown Chart and will also list the work that is completed, the work that has not been completed, and any work that was added after your sprint had started.

The sprint review is a meeting for sharing. The team is going to show what they've been able to ship in that sprint. Each of these sprints should produce a working part of the product that is known as an increment. This is a meeting that should contain a ton of feedback on the project and will include a brainstorming session so that the team can decide what they want to accomplish in the next phase or the next sprint.

Once the sprint is done, it is time to hold the retrospective meeting. For a two-week sprint, this is going to last about 90 minutes or so. This is the time for the team to inspect itself and how well it did. They will look at their own processes, the team interaction, the tools they used, and more to determine if there are any areas for improvement that need to be taken. You should also complete one of these retrospectives even when a team is doing really well to ensure that nothing is missed out on.

At the end of your sprint, you need to complete or close it out on Jira. If there are any issues that were not finished during the sprint for some reason, you can either move those back to your backlog, move these issues over to a future sprint, or move them to a new sprint that Jira can create for you right then if you would like.

At this point, you already know some of the basics of creating your own backlog with some user stories, how to organize those stories into sprints, how to start the sprint, and even how to hold the different Scrum ceremonies or meetings that are needed to make this project as successful as possible. After doing this process once, you have a good idea of how it all works and the steps that you need to take to do it over again. If you like the Scrum process, you can immediately get started on the next sprint, following the same steps that we have already discussed in this chapter over again!

Chapter 18: An Advanced Scrum Tutorial

The last chapter spent some time taking a look at how to follow the Scrum process. It was one of the basic examples but it has everything that you need to do a successful Scrum process. But there are times when you will need to go through and use some of the more advanced features that come with Scrum. This chapter is going to take a look at some of the more advanced practices that come with Scrum including using epics, customizing the workflow a bit, and using reports in the Jira Software.

Using Epics in the Backlog

There are times when your team needs to work on features that comprise a larger body of work. Any time that this happens, you should consider working with epics to planning out your work and grooming the backlog. Epics are basically large user stories that you are able to break up into parts that are more manageable.

Your epic can also span across more than one project if you want. If your team is working on some user stories that are supposed to build up to a larger user story and can turn into multiple projects, then it is time to use some epics. This makes it easier to track the project that you are working on.

To work on these epics, head to the backlog of your board and then expand out the epics panel simply by clicking on EPICS. This will help you to break up your projects into a few different parts that are easier to work with.

Customize the Workflow

If you have the default on when working in Jira, you will find that there are three statuses that your issues are going to move through. To do, in progress, and done. If this ends up being too simple for the kind of work that you want to do, then you can change up the statuses that you want to use in Jira to match the process that your team uses.

For example, if you are working on a project that is for software development, you could add in some new statuses including Code Review, Awaiting QA, and Ready to Merge. You can add in as many different statuses that you would like to use and Jira makes this as easy as possible. Just make the new parts work for the process that your team likes to work with.

Using the Velocity Chart

Another thing that you can work within your Scrum project is the velocity chart. Jira software is all about helping you get all of the potentials out of your team. When you use the velocity chart, you can see a summary of the work that your team is delivering at each and every sprint. This is some great information to have to help you see the progress and more.

You are able to use this information to help you predict the realistic amount of work that your team will be able to complete on future sprints. During the planning meetings for the sprint, your team can go through the visuals of what has happened in some of the previous sprints and the team's commitment versus what they are actually able to complete. Then they can take this information and come up with commitments that are realistic to what the team can actually do.

Using Wallboards

Another thing that you can use with your Scrum project is the Wallboards. With everything that is going on with each project, it is worth considering using one of these wallboards to ensure that your team is always up to speed, without having to go through all the paperwork and the rest of the information for the project. You can easily connect the computer to a TV monitor and then the dashboard with Jira will become a physical wallboard. You can then use some of the agile gadgets that are present in real time to help the team stay on the same page the whole project.

These are just a few of the advanced tools that you may want to use with your Scrum project. Remember that Scrum can always be adapted and changed to deal with and make your project easier to work with. Scrum is not supposed to be a difficult process. It is one that is meant to make the work of the team easier than ever before. If you find that these tools are great for your project management, then make sure you get the work completed as efficiently and productively as possible.

Conclusion

Thank you for making it through the end of *Scrum Project Management*. Let's hope it was informative and able to provide you with all of the tools you need to achieve your goals whatever they may be.

The next step is to decide whether or not you would like to add Scrum Project Management to your own business plan today. There are a lot of different frameworks that you can decide to implement into your business, but none are going to be as successful and easy to use as working with Scrum. This framework is simple, easy to learn, and will involve both a team and individual customers and their feedback into the whole process.

With Scrum, you are able to keep your costs down to a minimum. You know from the beginning how long a sprint is going to last and you will be able to determine the costs right at the beginning. This makes it easier to keep the costs as low as possible and can help you forecast into the future. You also keep the work into small teams, allowing them to share ideas and learn how to work with each other to get the project done. With lots of meetings, a clear idea of the tasks that need to be done and more, the Scrum Team is going to be able to get more done than ever before.

There are also plenty of opportunities for the customer to provide their own feedback about the product. With some of the traditional methods of making a product, the business would hope that they got a great idea, they would develop the whole thing, and then they would send it out to market. Sometimes the product would do well and the company would make a lot of profit. And other times, the product wouldn't do as well as hoped. This was a huge risk and kept a lot of great products from getting into the market.

With the help of Lean, Agile, and Scrum, the company can work slowly on a product taking in customer feedback along the way. The team can listen to what the customer is saying and will make the necessary changes as much as possible. Then, when the product is finally released to the market, there is a high amount of confidence that the product is going to do well because it is something that the customers will value.

This guidebook took the time to discuss these options for Scrum and so much more. This framework may seem a little bit difficult and complex in the beginning, but it really can make a big difference in how well your business works and the different products (and the value of the products) that you provide to your customers.

If you have ever considered implementing Scrum into your business or if you have considered changing up the developmental process of your company to make it more efficient overall, then it is time to take a look through this guidebook. It will provide you with all of the information that you need to make Scrum and all its features work well for your business.

Finally, if you found this book useful in any way, a review on Amazon is always appreciated!